A PORTRAIT OF ROMAN BRITAIN

A PORTRAIT OF
ROMAN BRITAIN

John Wacher

London and New York

First published 2000
by Routledge
11 New Fetter Lane, London EC4P 4EE

Simultaneously published in the USA and Canada
by Routledge
29 West 35th Street, New York, NY 10001

Routledge is an imprint of the Taylor & Francis Group

© 2000 John Wacher

Typeset in Garamond by
Exe Valley Dataset
Printed and bound in Great Britain by
TJ International Ltd,
Padstow, Cornwall

British Library Cataloguing in Publication Data
A catalogue record for this book is available from the British Library

Library of Congress Cataloging in Publication Data

Wacher, J.S.
  A portrait of Roman Britain/John Wacher
      p. cm.
  Includes bibliographical references (p. 125) and index.
      1. Great Britain—History—Roman period, 55 B.C.—449 A.D.
      2. Great Britain—Antiquities, Roman. 3. Romans—Great Britain. I. Title.
  DA145.W124 2000
  936.1'04—dc21   99–048121

ISBN 0–415–03321–7

CONTENTS

ILLUSTRATIONS

ACKNOWLEDGEMENTS

I am very grateful to Charles Smith for reading the draft of Chapter 1, and for correcting any errors of geology. Also to the York Archaeological Trust for making available the information on which the Appendix is based.

My thanks go to the following for providing illustrations and for giving permission for the reuse: Brian Simmons for fig. 4; Alan Bowman and the Haverfield Bequest for figs 37 and 39; Roger Tomlin for fig. 38; Barry Burnham for figs 32 and 40; Alan McWhirr and the Corinium Museum for figs 30 and 34; Peter Wilson for fig. 31; David Vale and FLARE for figs 20 and 21; Philip Crummy and Peter Froste for fig. 27; Paul Bennett, John Bowen and the Canterbury Archaeological Trust for fig. 26. Finally, Adam Sharpe again produced some excellent drawings for figs 1, 17, 18, 19, 31, and 37–40, while Barbara Kane once more manipulated a word processor with her usual skill.

Many of the photographs are my own, so any blemishes are attributable to me; likewise any contentious issues in the text.

John Wacher
Hayle
1999

INTRODUCTION
The Landscape as a Concept

The *Oxford English Dictionary* defines a landscape as a piece of inland scenery or a picture representing it. This book attempts to create a picture of the landscape during the period when most of the British Isles was part of the Roman Empire, though a picture not on canvas, but in words.

The scenery which we observe in Britain today, and which many conservationists seek to preserve, is seldom entirely 'natural'; indeed the word is something of a contradiction, for, ever since the earliest farmers sowed their primitive crops in the first woodland clearings, and built their dwellings alongside, people have been interfering with the British landscape. Consequently, any attempt to preserve what is here and now is but an interruption in a process of natural or human-influenced evolution; landscapes are constantly changing, the agents for change being as diverse as erosion, accumulation, vegetational growth and decay, and humanity. Undoubtedly the greatest factor has been humanity, and only in the bleakest hill country of the north, the south-west and Wales have humans had little impact, and even in these regions early attempts at mining or quarrying may have effected changes, while modern practices of burning heather and over-grazing by sheep have made significant alterations. In other parts of the country, excessive drainage and extraction of water are creating conditions unseen in antiquity, with the shrinkage of wetlands, the drying up of rivers and the consequent soil erosion and change in vegetational cover. Yet, despite the continual tampering with the visual appearance of the countryside, land so treated, but since abandoned, soon reverts to nature. Hence the outlines of prehistoric fields and earthworks, of Roman forts and roads, of deserted medieval villages and the defunct early workings of the industrial revolution still survive. When all is said and done, that evocative poem of Rudyard Kipling, 'The Land', sums it up. People come; they leave their imprint on the landscape and depart; the land remains in the hands of Old Hobden, changed and yet unchangeable.

Every landscape is comprised of three elements: form, colour and texture; three factors have created them: geology, climate and, most frequently, humanity.

Form, in an undeveloped environment, is provided by the characteristic shapes and distribution of trees and shrubs, whether singly or in a mass; by different types of grassland, heath or bog; by hills, cliff and rocky outcrops in upland areas; by dunes along the coast; and by rivers and streams. If humans have had a hand in shaping the landscape, these features can be supplemented by mounds, ditches, banks and other earthworks, and the occasional building, either extant or ruined. In the Roman landscape as it was, such buildings would have been comparatively few and far between, and would have ranged from the humble native farms and houses through all varieties of villas, each with their related structures such as granaries, barns and byres. Since buildings of all types at this period seldom rose above a ground-floor level, with, at best in most, only a single upper storey (although some tower-like wings have occasionally been identified), their visual impact on the form of the rural landscape would have been small. Other structures to be expected in the countryside would have been rural temples and shrines, perhaps associated with some prominent totem, such as a tree or rock. The plan of the Romano-Celtic temple lends itself to a central raised structure, and, since they were sometimes situated on high ground, as in abandoned hillforts, they will have exerted a more dominant effect. Other features would have included the occasional barrow, mausoleum or single graves situated often in groups near villas or alongside roads, especially just outside towns; and, of course, the roads themselves, often raised above the surrounding land on an agger, with their related works, such as ditches, milestones and bridges. Field boundaries consisting of banks, hedges or walls would have been comparatively ubiquitous, particularly in the so-called lowland zone.

The form of the Romano-British rural landscape today appears very different, sealed as it usually is below more recent accretions. Unless bodily removed or ploughed out, the aggers of roads and other earthworks often survive, but masonry buildings are at best represented by low grass-covered mounds over the reduced walls, and at worst by scatters of building stone or other debris in ploughed fields, often only to be properly appreciated by aerial survey.

The urban form would have been dictated primarily by buildings, although it is to be assumed that there would also have been trees and other vegetation; indeed, evidence for tree-root cavities has come from Leicester and Carlisle (p. 74). As in the countryside, most domestic and commercial buildings would have contained, at the most, only a single upper storey. Rising above them in the principal towns, though, would have been a range of public buildings, chief of which would have been the forum and basilica. The buildings round the piazza of the former were probably no more than single storey, but the basilica, a large aisled hall, would have risen well above them. Such evidence as we have from architectural fragments demonstrates the heights of these buildings, which would have dominated their towns. Other public buildings over-topping the general run of private construction would have been a theatre and/or an amphitheatre, with the latter situated usually on the fringes, the bath-house and possibly some temples. The bath-house, the hot rooms of which were normally vaulted, would have been placed to take advantage of the water supply and drainage. Later in the life of most towns in Britain, the provision of fortifications would have radically altered their visual appearances, with massive walls, often containing monumental gateways, surrounding the major parts of the built-up areas.

Colour and texture tend to vary with the seasons, as might be expected, and, as with form, are mainly provided by vegetation. In winter, and in areas where cultivation predominates, the prevailing colour is brown, highlighted by the residual green of pasture and evergreens. This will change in summer almost to a universal green, only varied by the different colours of individual species, with the intermediate phases of spring and autumn providing their own unique blends. Further subtle changes will be observed according to the time of day and the degree of exposure to sunlight. Given these constant, but ever changing, factors relating to colour, the landscape of Roman

Britain would have been basically similar to that of today, the only major differences being accounted for by buildings, but, even here, the use of local materials would have provided an element of continuity.

Similar seasonal variations will have occurred with texture, which in vegetation would have been provided by the distinctive leaf, branch and twig patterns of each species, according to the time of year. The texture of buildings would have come from the nature of the materials used in construction and would have been most discernible in the roofs, especially in single-storey buildings: tile, slate, thatch, turf, or even shingles, each with its own unique appearance.

Consequently, it can be appreciated that the visual aspect of Roman Britain would have been, as today, composed of a wide range of variables, many of which would change according to the seasons.

1

THE EFFECT OF GEOLOGY, CLIMATE AND HUMANITY

Behind and beneath the variables of form, colour and texture, as set out in the Introduction, was another set of factors consisting of geology, climate and humanity.

The basic geology of Britain (fig. 1) follows a line running very roughly north-east to south-west, with the older rocks lying on the north-western side. These older rocks form the regions of the south-west peninsula, Wales, the Pennines, Lake District and Scotland. The younger rocks on the other side of the line contain mainly the limestones and chalks, together with a good deal of alluvium. Consequently, as a general rule, but one with many local exceptions, the soils to the north-west are often acidic, while those to the south-east are mostly alkaline and are also better drained. Each supports its own brand of characteristic vegetation.

Starting therefore from the south-east and working systematically north and west, we come first to the chalk ridges of the North and South Downs, extending from Kent and Sussex respectively as far west as Wiltshire and Dorset, and terminating on the Channel coast in the cliffs of the South Foreland and Beachy Head. Being easily weathered, they tend to present a smooth, rounded surface, with the steepest gradients on the scarps of the south side of the North Downs and north side of the South Downs. They are separated by a wide area centred on the hump of the Weald, consisting of calcareous sandstones, limestones, clays, gravels and sands. The North Downs drain northwards towards the Thames estuary, giving rise to the river valleys of the Stour, the Mole, the Wey and the Medway, which cut through the chalk also to drain the north Weald in the same direction. The Stour, which now enters the sea on the Channel coast north of Sandwich, in Roman times bifurcated at the Wantsum with a second arm entering the North Sea west of Margate, so separating the chalk of the Isle of Thanet from the mainland. In the same way, the Medway divides in two, to embrace the Isle of Sheppey, before entering the Thames estuary. The central beds of the Weald drain to the east in the general area of what is now Romney Marsh, a coastal accretion composed largely of shingle beds and alluvium which has mostly formed since the Roman period. To the south, the rivers Arun, Adur and Ouse have cut valleys through the South Downs to the Channel coast.

There are some places on the North Downs which are capped or penetrated by clay-with-flints and sands, giving rise to local areas of acidic soil, and supporting a heath-like vegetation and other lime-hating plants. They also support a heavier tree growth along the top of the ridge (fig. 2), today consisting mainly of beech and hazel, with some oak, hornbeam and ash, so giving them their characteristic appearance and forming the chief distinction from the South Downs, where such woodland is rare, and

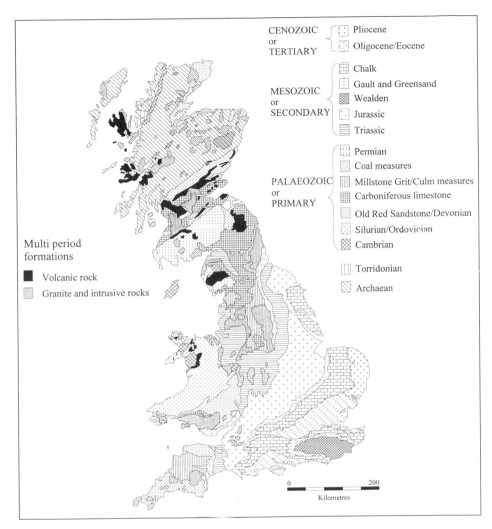

Figure 1 Geological map of Britain (after B. Jones and D. Mattingly).

tends to form isolated clumps (fig. 3). In Roman times there was probably less beech and hornbeam and more oak and probably birch, which would also have extended across the valley floors. It is difficult to say precisely what type of vegetation the exposed chalk of both Downs supported in antiquity. It probably varied from rough grass to a scrub of blackthorn, hawthorn, field maple, dogwood, wayfaring tree, buckthorn, with perhaps some wild cherry, spindleberry, yew and holly, and an undergrowth of brambles, honeysuckle and traveller's joy. It is interesting that the onset of myxomatosis in the 1950s and 1960s caused many areas of uncultivated grassland on the Downs to revert to this type of vegetation. The remaining flora would probably have not been much different in Roman times from that observed on uncultivated downs today, with an abundance of wild flowers and grasses according to the local habitat. Where open areas exist on the clay-with-flints, it is not unusual and yet something of a surprise to find

Figure 2 The Stour gap in the North Downs near Canterbury: a piece of chalk downland country. The top of the far ridge is covered by woodland, in contrast to the South Downs.

patches of heather, bracken and other lime-hating plants. One such place on the North Downs still supports a flourishing colony of Medium Wintergreen (*Pyrola media*), normally a flower of northern woods and wet acid moors.

The clay soils of the Weald supported heavy afforestation, primarily of oak, with the patches of sands and gravels covered with a lighter vegetation of birch, pine, broom and gorse, with sometimes large intervening areas of heathland. Unlike the Downs, there are rocky outcrops, mainly of sandstone, such as High Rocks at Tunbridge Wells, but otherwise the landscape consists of smooth, gently undulating hills, which rise in places to over 250 m, notably at Leith Hill, south of Dorking, and Ashdown Forest.

The western extremities of the North and South Downs eventually merge into a large area of chalk downlands in north Hampshire and Wiltshire which terminate in Salisbury Plain, the former by the thin ridge of the Hog's Back, west of Guildford. Another area of chalk extends south-west from Salisbury Plain into Dorset, while from the north flank the third major chalk downs in England, the Chilterns, emerge in a north-easterly direction. Although starting as a prominent range of some height, they gradually decline to rolling, prairie-like country in east Hertfordshire and north Essex, until in Suffolk and Norfolk they are almost entirely submerged in places by thick beds of sands, gravels and clays, which, unlike the remainder, support an acidic vegetation. Otherwise, although perhaps more wooded than the Downs, their visual appearance would have been very similar.

The chalk which forms the Chilterns is breached by the Wash, before re-emerging as the Lincolnshire Wolds, being breached again by the river Humber and then on to become the Yorkshire Wolds, before finally terminating at the Vale of Pickering and in the jutting headland of Flamborough Head. The entire range of chalklands from

Figure 3 The South Downs behind Worthing, with Chanctonbury Ring marked by the distant copse. The remainder is bare of woodland in contrast to the North Downs.

Wiltshire to Yorkshire are bisected by numerous valleys, some of which are now dry, but which, as today, probably supported extensive areas of calcereous woodland.

Between the chalk ridges of the North Downs and the Chilterns lies the broad area of the Thames valley, which extends outwards along the north Kent coast and up the coast of Essex. Geologically, these are some of the most recent formations in Britain with their base of London clay. There are also areas of sands and gravels overlying the clay, with others emerging from beneath its edges, as well as alluvium. The landscape presents a gently rolling appearance with some higher areas and plateaux. In prehistoric and early Roman times, much would have been heavily forested with oak and possibly elm, ash and lime. The wetter areas of the river valleys, such as the Thames itself and its numerous tributaries, probably supported willow and alder. For the first time, in the Roman period, we have literary evidence for the vegetational cover north of the Thames. Caesar in his account of his second expedition to Britain refers to Cassivellaunus' army 'hiding in dense thickets', probably mainly of blackthorn and hawthorn with an undergrowth of brambles and other entwining plants; the spines and thorns on all these, and possibly also wild rose, are just as effective as barbed-wire entanglements in detaining an attacking force. He also relates that Casivellaunus' main stronghold, somewhere in north Hertfordshire and often identified as the oppidum at Wheathampstead, was protected by forests and marshes. Nevertheless, there were also clearings, lanes and pathways, through and over which chariot attacks were delivered against the Roman army.

The middle reaches of the Thames valley, in Surrey and Hampshire, are covered with a thick bed of acid sands and gravels, which even today support extensive heaths, accompanied by birch and pine.

The river itself and its tributaries would have been bordered by alluvium, which in low-lying places was probably marsh or fen supporting reed beds, willow, alder, plus other aquatic or semi-aquatic plants. These areas were no doubt flooded from time to time, although it is important to remember that, without control of the river's flow by weirs and locks as today, the water would have been able to escape to the sea much more quickly and therefore levels would have fluctuated considerably. The tidal flow in the Thames is now constrained by Teddington lock; before its construction, the tide could well have reached farther upstream, although it is unlikely, but it was certainly tidal as far up as the City of London in Roman times. There is both literary and archaeological evidence for the existence of marshes (presumably salt marshes) on the south shore at Southwark, much of which was flooded at high tide. But even if the tide had not then reached as far as it does today, it would have caused backing-up of the freshwater flow, and so twice-daily fluctuations in the level.

The two other main estuaries on the east coast, which lie broadly within chalk areas, are the Wash and the Humber, although the latter is also associated with the oolites. Various investigations carried out by drainage authorities in conjunction with archaeologists have shown that the area of the Wash was considerably larger in late prehistoric and Roman times than it is today. Much of it would have been salt marsh and mud banks with a number of low islands not flooded at high tide. As with the lower Thames estuary, there would no doubt have been extensive reed beds along the tidal margins, and willows and alder on the higher land. The Fens can be divided into two parts: those composed largely of silt and those where peat is uppermost. The former (fig. 4), when drained, makes excellent agricultural land, but the latter, unless subjected to massive artificial treatment, does not have the same properties. There is evidence to show that, under Hadrian, an extensive land drainage scheme was instituted (p. 122).

The lower reaches of the Humber would have been not unlike the area around the Wash, with tidal mud flats and salt marsh. The estuary, though, is more restricted higher upstream, where it passes through both chalk and oolite; however, bands of alluvium, known locally as Humber warp, flank it on both sides. Much of this has been brought in by the tide from erosion of the Yorkshire coast and it also forms islands and massive, constantly shifting mud banks in the river, which even today are something of a hazard to navigation. The large area above the estuary, usually called Humber head, and where the river divides to become the Trent and the Ouse, were wetlands, supporting a typical marshland vegetation. The country here is characterized, as in the Fens, by its excessive flatness.

North and west of the Chilterns, the Lincolnshire and Yorkshire Wolds, Salisbury Plain and the Dorset chalklands, lies an area of sands and clays, which, while comparatively restricted at both ends, widens out in the middle. Although generally undulating in character, there are some ranges of comparatively high hills, such as those in the region of Little Brickhill (Beds.). The varying soil types also give rise to different vegetational cover. The clays were probably heavily wooded, again with oak, ash and elm predominating, but the lighter and more acid, sandy soils supported heathland, birch and pine. Areas of gravel are also known throughout the area, more especially in the upper reaches of the various river valleys such as that of the Thames. Less acid than the sands, they were probably covered with light forest or scrub of oak, elm, ash, hazel, blackthorn, hawthorn and similar trees and bushes. The river margins, always liable to

Figure 4 The Fens at Potterhanworth (Lincs.), with the Car Dyke in the centre (reproduced
by the kind permission of Brian Simmons).

flood, would have seen marshy areas with reed beds, probably interspersed with willow
and alder.

Beyond the band of clays which fringes this area on its north and western sides, a
gradual ascent is made up the dip-slope of the oolites, to the area generally known as
the Jurassic zone. At the southern end in Dorset, these oolites curl round the west end
of the central southern chalklands towards the east, giving rise to the headlands of
Portland Bill and St Alban's Head. The geology here is very confused, with the result
that soil types become mixed, with patches of an acidic nature being interspersed
among a generally alkaline background. The oolites reach their highest point in the
Cotswolds of Gloucestershire (fig. 5), gradually declining and thinning towards the
north until in Lincolnshire and Yorkshire only a narrow ridge survives up to Market
Weighton, in the latter county. From there they then reappear to flank the south-
western side of the Vale of Pickering before merging with the massif of the North
Yorkshire Moors. The scarp side of this ridge is more heavily indented with combs and
dry valleys, which are floored with lias clays, than the dip-slope, although the latter is
the source of a number of major rivers, such as the Thames and the Nene and, in
Yorkshire, the Derwent.

As with the Downs, the Jurassic hills tend to be smooth and rounded, with a good
deal of undulation but often with somewhat steeper gradients. In many places they are
capped by a layer of fragmented limestone and clay, which can support a thin vegetation of grass, lime-loving plants and scrub of a similar nature to that observed on the
chalks. The valleys are more heavily wooded, and once supported large forests, such as
the now sadly depleted Rockingham Forest in Northamptonshire. In this middle
region the rock is highly ferruginous and has been mined for iron ore certainly since
Roman times.

Figure 5 The Cotswold scarp from the villa at Witcombe (Glos.).

Beyond the Jurassic zone to the north and west, the geology of Britain becomes much more fragmented. In the west Midlands and extending in the east up the Trent valley and on into the Vale of York, and in the west up the Lancashire coast, are large areas of heavy clays based on the Triassic series, presenting a low, gently undulating profile of nearly neutral or slightly acid soils. It used to be assumed that most of this area was heavily forested in prehistoric times, as it probably was, but there are also parts, especially in the flood plains of the rivers, where the clays are capped with gravels and sands, giving rise to a well-drained lighter vegetation which could more easily be cleared and settled. There are also in some places exposures of earlier rocks from the carboniferous series, allied with some intrusions of an igneous nature, such as those in Charnwood (Leics.) and between Birmingham and Wolverhampton. These levels contain the Midlands coal fields of Leicestershire, Warwickshire and Staffordshire.

While it is true to say that Britain south and east of, and including, the Jurassic zone consists mainly of alkaline soils with pockets of an acidic nature, the reverse is the case to the north and west. This remaining area of older rocks divides naturally into five regions: the Pennines, which terminate in the Cheviots of southern Scotland, the Highland massif, the Lake District, Wales and the south-west peninsula. Although limestones, such as the carboniferous, dolomitic and magnesian, occur in some of these regions, they are more often than not covered in thick beds of peat, which shrouds their alkaline nature. This difference between north-west and south-east has also produced the distinctive highland and lowland areas of the country, with the best cultivatable, alkaline soil lying in the latter, while the former was more suitable for grazing. But the highland area was also intersected by numerous river valleys, which, probably once wooded, provided a limited amount of ground for early settlement and cultivation on the river terraces. Since the rocks were harder than chalk and oolite,

Figure 6 The western Pennines north of Settle (Yorks.). The hill dominating the background is Ingleborough, crowned by an Iron Age hillfort.

they lend themselves to more dramatic landscapes with high hills, sharp gradients and exposed rock-faces.

The southern end of the Pennines is dominated by the Peak District, largely of carboniferous limestone but with numerous igneous intrusions, providing a somewhat mixed vegetation, but mostly open moorland of grass and heath. Beyond to the north and east lies a broad swathe of limestone country which terminates quite abruptly along the line of Airedale. This area is separated from a similar one on the west side of the Pennines by the central spine of millstone grits (fig. 6), of an acid nature, which continues on northwards before sweeping round the southern edge of the Cheviots and terminating in the North Sea off the Northumberland coast.

The Pennines is also the area where bogs and mosses begin to occur at all levels, producing characteristic wetland flora, based on thick beds of peat. In the lower-lying areas these become raised mosses, which are now sadly in decline due to excessive land drainage. Outside the bogs, but still in the wetter areas, the three main varieties of heather – ling, purple heather and the cross-leaved heath – are accompanied by the several forms of bilberry, an edible berry, which in higher areas replaces the ubiquitous bramble as a source of food. In some remaining places in the higher, northern part of the Pennines and in the Cheviots beyond are a few survivals of an alpine vegetation, left behind by the last glaciation.

The river systems of the eastern Pennines, as far north as Swaledale, flow to form the two main rivers, Ouse and Trent, in turn giving rise to the Vale of York and the Trent valley, before combining in the Humber. North of Swaledale, the Tees, Wear and Tyne individually drain into the North Sea. There are fewer rivers on the west side, since the drainage pattern is interrupted by the Lake District, and consists mainly of the Mersey, the Ribble and, in the north, the Eden. Each flows to the sea through wide estuaries and extensive flood plains, with characteristic marshlands and reedbeds, not unlike those surrounding the Thames, Wash and Humber and probably originally supporting similar vegetation.

The Vale of Eden partly separates the Pennines from the Lake District before becoming the Solway Firth. The landscape of the Lake District is unlike almost any other part of Britain, with its deeply fissured hills, abrupt inclines, bare summits and numerous lakes. The geology is complex, caused by large areas of extrusive and intrusive volcanic rocks which have produced the contorted strata. It is likely, though, that in antiquity the margins of the lakes supported broad-leaved woodland, as indeed many do today, while the uplands were probably a mix of thin grassland with patches of heath.

The Cheviots present large areas of bare, open, rolling hill country with mainly alkaline soils, although there are also outcrops of sandstones and intrusive igneous rocks where grassland is replaced by heath. North of them in the basin containing the two main rivers, the Forth and the Clyde, lies more broken country based on complex geological features, containing carboniferous limestones, millstone grits, sandstones and volcanic intrusions, supporting a mixed vegetation according to the nature of the underlying soil, which is mainly acid. North of the river valleys the foothills of the Highlands begin in Strathearn, and from there northwards again lie the Highlands proper, consisting mainly of igneous and metamorphic rocks. Heather-clad moorland is the predominating cover of the uplands, although numerous glens and locks support both deciduous and coniferous trees, among which oak, birch and the Scots pine are the most significant. Some areas still support today carefully guarded remnants of the ancient forests of the latter species, but we cannot be certain now how much ground they originally covered.

Many of the estuaries and sea locks in the lower-lying areas, especially the Clyde, Forth and Tay, contain deposits of alluvium, while the coastal margins in these areas are fringed by extensive sand dunes, often of considerable height. Being composed in many cases of crushed shells, they are calcareous in nature and therefore support a lime-loving vegetation, in marked contrast to their surroundings.

The Roman army seems never to have penetrated far into the Scottish Highlands, contenting themselves with occasional operations around the eastern, coastal fringe as far as the Moray Firth, although it is said that the navy circumnavigated the north coast in the late first century. For the remaining, comparatively short time when they occupied the area beyond the Forth–Clyde line, they halted on the north edge of Strathearn coinciding with the southern fringe of the Highlands.

The landscape of Wales presents a very similar picture to parts of Scotland. The central hills are divided roughly into two blocks by the valley of the river Severn, but otherwise present a picture of open moorland, often intersected by smaller valleys. The highest part lies around Snowdonia in the north-west, an area affected by volcanic activity in the geological past with both intrusive and extrusive rocks, a pattern which is repeated in the south-west. The coast bordering the Severn estuary, together with its tributaries, is covered with deep areas of alluvium, which, further west along the Bristol Channel, become sand dunes of a calcareous nature, a phenomenon which is repeated along the shores of Cardigan Bay and the Menai Straits.

The next region to be considered is the south-west peninsula of Somerset, Devon and Cornwall, which lies west of the Jurassic zone; the latter terminates in Lyme Bay in the remarkable series of cliffs and hills bordering Bridport.

Figure 7 Taunton Vale from the Blackdown Hills, with the Quantocks in the background.

Somerset is a diverse county geologically, bounded by oolites to the east, which produce the noted Bath stone. These hills, as with the Cotswolds further north, are very broken along their western edge with numerous combs and outliers, giving rise to a calcareous vegetation, and with the lower-lying areas heavily wooded. Between them and the Severn estuary is an area of undulating hills composed of varying carboniferous rocks allied with cornbrash as far as the shore-line, which, as with its counterpart on the north shore, is buried in deep alluvium. The south-western boundary is formed by the hump of the Mendips, composed mainly of magnesian limestone; beyond them is the flat, low-lying area of the Somerset levels, from which erupt the remarkable, isolated hills of Brent Knoll and Glastonbury Tor.

The Somerset levels are an area of waterlogged fen country, now largely drained by agriculture and peat extraction. Originally, they would have been subject to repeated flooding, producing thick beds of peat and supporting a vegetation similar to the fens of East Anglia: reed beds, scrub of alder and willow, and, on the higher parts, probably elm and ash. The levels extend inland as far as the oolites, while on the Severn shore they terminate in the broad estuary of the river Parrett, with its sand and mud flats. On the south-western side they rise up to the Quantocks, a dominant ridge of sandstones, now heavily forested on the dip-slope, but with open heath and moorland along the crest and scarp (fig. 7). A valley separates these hills from the outliers of Exmoor, one of the principal upland features of the south-west.

Exmoor, unlike the other remaining moorlands in the peninsula, is based mainly on sandstones and carboniferous rocks, supporting a partly acid vegetation of heath and allied plants. Unlike the other moors of the south-west, which are of volcanic origin, Exmoor presents a smoother and more rounded profile, and lacks the characteristic granite tors of the former; its fringes along the Bristol Channel, however, form high and precipitous cliffs.

Figure 8 A granite tor.

Dartmoor is the highest and largest of the moors in the remaining part of the region, being composed of rugged intrusive igneous rocks, which in places erupt as craggy masses known as tors (fig. 8). The vegetation consists of grass and heather moorland with areas of scrub and bracken in the valleys around the edges, some of which also support woods of coniferous and deciduous trees. The moor is also noted for its bogs, some of which are of a considerable size and depth. East and south of Dartmoor lie areas of sandstones, which on the western edge of Lyme Bay produce the red cliffs around Dawlish and the remarkable bright red soil which can be seen in arable fields. Further east still and beyond the river Exe is a very broken region of greensands, with, in places, surviving uneroded outliers of the Dorset chalks. Consequently, the vegetation is very mixed, but includes large wooded areas of oak, ash and beech.

The remainder of Devon and also north Cornwall is an undulating region based on carboniferous rocks. At one time probably heavily wooded, it is now mostly pasture.

Cornwall is dominated by the four major areas of intrusive igneous rock: Bodmin Moor, Hensbarrow Downs, Carnmenellis and the high moors of west Penwith, interspersed with areas of lowland mosses, most of which have now been drained (fig. 9). Although geologically of a different nature, the Lizard peninsula falls within the same category; it appears as a comparatively level plateau, broken by coastal combs and supporting an acid vegetation of heath, grass and bracken, in all respects similar to the high moors. The remainder of the county is also covered by acid soils with the exception of some coastal fringes and estuaries, especially on the north coast, where, as in Scotland and Wales, there are considerable accumulations of calcareous sands (fig. 10).

The last area to be considered is that in south Hampshire and the Isle of Wight. As with most parts of the south and east, the geological formations are comparatively

Figure 9 A lowland moss, which is gradually being invaded by scrub.

recent, and on the mainland are composed of gravel and pebble beds with some sands and clays. They are intersected by three major tidal estuaries: Poole Harbour, Southampton Water and Portsmouth Harbour. Today they support one of England's largest and best known forests – the New Forest – and also extensive heathlands, being principally acid in nature. There are also marshy parts and the low-lying estuaries are flanked by mud banks and flats exposed at low tide. The Isle of Wight possesses an east–west spine and southern core of chalk and greensand with associated clays and marls and therefore supports a varied vegetation according to the soil type; the banded sands in the cliffs at Alum Bay are particularly noteworthy. The lower-lying northern part of the island is made up of clays and marls.

If geology forms the bones of the landscape, then climate moulds and creates the flesh, both in the topography and vegetation. We should not be surprised today at the onset of what appears to be global warming. It has often happened before, as well as cooling, and certainly several times within the last millennium. The climate is quite capable of altering itself without any help from the human race. The forces at work in nature can dwarf all the puny contributions made by man. What is lacking in most modern studies is a sense of proportion and historicity. Britain was particularly affected by a consequence of climate change, since it is entirely surrounded by the sea: the rise and fall in sea level, with the resulting erosion or build-up of coastal regions. A rise in sea level will lead to water being backed up in rivers, so also affecting areas far inland, as will also a fall in the reverse direction. Neither climate nor sea level have ever been static; they have always been changing and will no doubt continue to be so far into the future. Even in the Roman period in Britain, they are thought to have changed quite markedly.

Absolute certainty of the climate of Roman Britain cannot be assessed, but it seems likely that the same general trends as today were in force. Caesar's brief mentions of

Figure 10 Upton Towans, a coastal dune formation rising in places to over 70 m, east of the river Hayle (Cornwall). Similar coastal dunes occur in parts of both Wales and Scotland.

sudden storms in the Channel, westerly and south-westerly winds and equinoctial gales would make it appear that Britain was then subject to prevailing westerlies, depressions, and, in the calmer periods he mentions, ridges of high pressure; in other words, the mixture as we know it today. We can also infer from the numerous river-systems of Britain that there was always a good rainfall. It seems probable, therefore, that the main climatic differences between the east and west of the country applied then, as today, with the south-west, Wales, England west of the Pennines and the west of Scotland tending to be wetter and milder than the east, with the driest areas being concentrated around the flatter lands of East Anglia, Lincolnshire and north Kent; the lack of major hills here is the main cause of the minimal precipitation.

Frost, wind, rain and sun all play a part in soil and rock erosion. If water in rocky fissures freezes, it expands, thus causing fragmentation when, in the following thaw and with the action of rain and wind, pieces become detached. The same effect can be caused on sun-heated strata being rapidly cooled by rain or night frost. Softer rocks, usually with a higher water content, are more susceptible to these effects: hence the gradual retreat of the chalk and limestone cliffs of southern England, and the clay cliffs of the east coast. Running water from rainfall, or streams and rivers, can also cause erosion, the products of which are carried downstream, with the finer particles travelling furthest and often as far as the river's mouth, where they are deposited as silt or mud banks. In this way climate has a gradual effect on the topography of the landscape, tending to flatten out the highspots and fill in the lower-lying areas.

The heavier rainfall in the west leads to a greener, lusher vegetation, especially in the valleys; but this effect is to some extent counteracted by the stronger winds which

Figure 11 An ancient woodland of stunted, mature oak and ash trees near the cliffs of the north Cornish coast. Similar woods, where trees are dwarfed by the winds, can be found on Dartmoor, and may once have covered much more of the higher lands of the south-west.

produce a barer, bleaker landscape on the uplands, with few mature trees; they are often bent almost horizontal by the prevailing winds. Similarly in places in the west country there are woodlands of diminutive oaks and ashes, stunted in height by the weather and growing laterally instead of upwards (fig. 11).

Variations in the world's climate cause changes in sea level, according to how much ice is locked in the polar icecaps. These fluctuations have been ever present and have caused marked changes in the British coastline. In recent geological time they have left the raised beaches stranded high-and-dry above the water. More recently still they have caused the silting of the Wantsum Channel between Kent and Thanet, the creation of the Fens, Somerset levels, Dungeness and Romney Marsh, and the erosion of the Yorkshire and Lincolnshire coasts, with their mythology of 'drowned towns'. The remarkable power of the sea is demonstrated frequently on the north Cornish coast where parts can be stripped of 3 m of sand overnight in a northerly gale, only for it to return the following night if the wind changes direction. The easterly creep of shingle along the Channel coast, apart from the great headland at Dungeness, covered the fine sand of Sandwich Bay with shingle in a matter of twenty to thirty years. If Caesar landed at Walmer, which is commonly supposed, the beach on which he landed was probably very different from the steeply shelving shingle banks which are there today. He refers to the enemy knowing all the shallows; there are none now at high tide, and it is more likely then to have been a gently shelving beach of sand, as was the neighbouring Sandwich Bay until only a few decades ago. But all the evidence so far collected would suggest that, in Iron Age and early Roman times, mean sea level was somewhat lower than it is today. However, it began to rise in the fourth century and by the end of that century was higher than today. This marine transgression had a considerable effect on lower-lying coastal sites, causing some to be abandoned or restricted in use.

The third principal factor in moulding the landscape was the work of the human race. It probably started with the earliest farmers in the Neolithic period, or even before, clearing patches in the extensive forests and scrublands which covered Britain, and has continued ever since, so that the landscape we see today is mainly the artificial creation of human activity. The forests were not then the neat, managed woodlands that we know today, but vast, tangled impenetrable tracts, with a density now difficult to imagine; home to bear, wild boar and wolves, they were at first an insurmountable barrier. Only on the fringes could the forest be cleared for primitive farming, when the first need of these people would have been demarcation boundaries to proclaim ownership and more importantly, to keep stock from wandering outside the enclosure or into arable crops. By using green wood to construct these fences, a proportion probably took root and grew, so creating the earliest hedges, which may have been amplified by a bank or ditch. In places where wood was scarce and stone abundant, drystone walls would have replaced hedges. Sometimes these took the form of large slabs set upright, and in west Cornwall their remnants can still be seen, dating probably to the Bronze Age or early Iron Age. On Dartmoor and Bodmin Moor similar enclosures still exist as part of the landscape.

So began the clearance of Britain's natural vegetation. By the Iron Age, large tracts of land had been so treated, especially on the lighter soils of the south-east, the downlands of Wessex, the Jurassic zone and in the river valleys of the west Midlands. By the time Caesar arrived in Britain, sufficient land was under cultivation for him to be able to rely on local foraging for part of his army's rations. Moreover, Strabo, writing at about the turn of BC/AD, records grain as a British export, which would imply a surplus of production and sufficient arable, presumably in Essex and Hertfordshire, to produce it. This area is highly suitable for cereal production, as the prairies beloved by modern agriculture now show; such methods inevitably lead to soil erosion, and further alterations in the landscape.

Apart from clearances for fields, others obviously had to be made for settlements. From the Bronze Age onwards, these made their impact on the landscape and today can be seen as surface features of low banks and ditches. The houses themselves, though, leave little visible trace, being built of timber; but in the highland areas, with ample stone, low walls were often constructed as bases for the timber superstructures. In steeply sloping areas, platforms and scoops were dug to create more level ground, and many of these features still survive as hut circles in the Pennines, Cheviots and the south-west, among other places.

Visual evidence for settlement sites may be slight, but the same cannot be said for burials. Barrows of various shapes and forms began to dot the landscape from the Neolithic onwards and large groups are still discernible in many places, especially on the higher ground in Wessex. Almost all have been eroded by the weather to some degree, but originally they must have been prominent features, so much so that Roman roads were sometimes aligned upon them.

It was during the late Bronze Age and early Iron Age that the first major impacts were made on the visual appearance of Britain, with the construction of hillforts and allied defensive enclosures. Although scarce in the south-east, East Anglia and east

Midlands, they cluster thickly in Wessex, the south-west, the Severn valley, Welsh Marches and central Midlands. They often began life as simple ditched and palisaded enclosures, although as time passed most were strengthened with the addition of massive earth or rock ramparts, often of multiple form. Many survive today in commanding hilltop positions, as the most characteristic part of the Iron Age landscape. Their construction must also represent considerable woodland clearance, since large quantities of timber would have been required. Such land, once cleared, could then have been put to agricultural use.

During the immediate pre-Roman Iron Age, another type of even larger fortified enclosure appeared, although they were fewer in number than the hillforts. They were the oppida, in which great areas of land were enclosed within massive dyke systems, such as at Colchester, Verulamium, Bagendon and Stanwick. Individual dykes did not always enclose the whole area, but stopped, for no apparent reason that can be seen today, in open countryside. This type of fortification would have provided the best defence primarily against chariots, which surprised Caesar when he met them on his arrival in Britain, since this form of warfare had become outmoded on the Continent. That being so, it is probably best to assume that gaps in the dyke systems were more than likely heavily wooded or of a marshy nature; both would have impeded chariot actions. It would seem, therefore, that not all areas within these oppida were cleared of trees; some forests remained, possibly for fattening pigs, while other cleared parts would have provided both pasture and cultivation alongside farms, several of which could have existed within the enclosures. Consequently, we can see these oppida as largely self-sufficient communities, usually with a tribal leader at their centres.

The arrival of the Roman army in AD 43 set in motion drastic changes to the countryside, many of which are still with us today in the positioning of towns, villages and road alignments. Indeed, the changes introduced during the 350 or so years of occupation were probably not matched again until the industrial revolution, with the invention of the steam engine, and later the internal combustion engine. We can only imagine the appearance of the British landscape now had the Romans possessed either or both of these two sources of power!

The first priorities of the army in Britain would have been food and timber. There was probably already a surplus of the former, and an increase in production could have been achieved with little extra effort in the south-eastern part of the country where, to begin with, most of the army was stationed. Timber, primarily for building forts, was another matter and a systematic felling programme would have been initiated, most likely using the heavily forested areas of the Weald.

It has been calculated that the single legionary fortress at Inchtuthil required some 16,000 m^3 of structural timber, and that one hectare of natural forest will only supply 9 m^3 by clear felling. Yet nearly a hundred auxiliary forts and at least six legionary fortresses were built within the first thirty or so years after the invasion, plus various other installations, such as vexillation fortresses. This could amount to close on 300,000 m^3 or 33,000 ha (330 km^2) of forest. Although this seems a very large figure, it is in fact only equivalent to about one-twentieth of the area of the Weald, which, all the evidence suggests, was not clear-felled at this time. The remainder of the first century, however, saw at least another hundred auxiliary forts and three more legionary fortresses built, probably equivalent to about another 200,000 m^3 or just over 200 km^2 But that was not the end. During the next hundred years, two new frontier lines were constructed, plus other forts and installations, although by now stone was also being employed; some earlier forts were rebuilt. There is, though, an unanswerable question as to how much timber was salvaged for reuse, and here opinion is divided. Certainly the Roman army took care to dismantle forts after they ceased to be occupied, but how far this salvaged timber then travelled to new sites is disputed. Even allowing for this factor, the army was responsible for clearing a minimum of 500 km^2 of woodland during the first 150 years of occupation. If we then add the requirements of the newly founded towns, villages and farms over the same period, it seems likely that the figure would approach 1,000 km^2 However and wherever this was done, and given that some regeneration probably took place, it cannot but have made a profound change to the landscape.

The second major change to the countryside would have been the construction of an arterial road system. Trackways undoubtedly existed in the Iron Age, mainly using higher, and therefore more lightly covered ground, such as the Icknield Way on the Chilterns. Meandering gently along the hills, their impact on the visual appearance of the land they traversed would have been minimal. But the new roads, with their straight courses cutting across the contours, their side ditches, raised profiles and the quarry pits along the edges, would have impinged more heavily. It is clear that the surveyors made careful reconnaissance to select the best alignments. For instance, Watling Street in the south Midlands heads straight for Watford Gap, near Rugby, so avoiding the steeper gradients on either side. It could not have been a better choice, since the same line was ultimately closely adopted by the main trunk road (A5), the Grand Union Canal, the main west coast railway line to Scotland and finally by the M1 motorway; all are situated here within a span of a few hundred metres. A good deal of argument has arisen about how the Roman alignments were so accurately surveyed, without any fully acceptable conclusion being reached.

The establishment of some dozen or more legionary and vexillation fortresses, nearly two hundred auxiliary forts and other military installations, twenty-one major and over fifty minor towns, with numerous smaller villages, in an area stretching from the south coast to the edge of the Scottish Highlands will also have had a considerable impact on the landscape. The changes would not be restricted to the area of the fort or town itself, but would extend outwards to embrace the surrounding countryside. Forts and fortresses would require grazing for horses, and hay meadows for fodder, and, as time went on, also for cultivation. Hay was being gathered from as far away as 15–20 km from York while a single quingenary ala of cavalry needed 360 ha of grazing. Moreover, most military installations, which were in existence for any length of time, attracted civil settlements, often occupying considerable areas of land.

It is probable that towns which developed in conjunction with existing Iron Age settlements were sited on land that had already been cleared of woodland and scrub. Since many of these towns also started as villages beside the early forts of the Julio-Claudian period, the same would apply to the latter, although forts were usually placed near, but often a few kilometres away from, their Iron Age counterparts.

Early forts, towns and villages would all contribute to the visual appearance of the landscape, providing additional forms, colour and texture. Since most buildings at this stage were constructed of timber and seldom rose above ground-floor level, the impact would have been small. A bath-house, where one existed, would probably have been the most prominent feature, being constructed of stone or brick, or a combination of both. The timber frames of other buildings were clad with daub (puddled clay) and there is abundant evidence that the exterior surfaces were lime-washed to provide protection from the weather. Colour would, therefore, have varied from pristine white for newly treated walls, through all shades of grey or green for more weathered examples, or for those where algae grew. In the south and east, roofs were often tiled, giving vibrant splashes of red to the scene; thatch or possibly shingles, while providing texture, would have produced a more muted colour scheme. Stone slates, in areas with suitable material, were normally diamond shaped, with the roofs taking on a scale-like appearance, while the colour varied according to the nature of the stone; but all would have with time accumulated a growth of lichen or moss so modifying the effect.

By the middle of the second century, many changes had been incorporated in the structures of both forts and towns. Most of the former had been given masonry defences and internal buildings, while in the major towns the growth of public buildings, such as forums, basilicas, baths, theatres, amphitheatres and temples, nearly always now built in stone, will have altered the skyline to a considerable degree. It is claimed today that an urban skyline is as good an identifying factor for a town as a fingerprint, and the same was probably true of the Roman period. Most of the major public buildings would have risen above the level of domestic and commercial premises, even though the latter may now have extended to an upper storey, and also been wholly or partly rebuilt in masonry. The basilica, placed near the centre of the town, would have been the most eye-catching building and would have dominated its surroundings in much the same way as cathedrals did from the middle ages right up to the present century; only with the accelerated construction of high-rise blocks and tower buildings has this changed. Second would have been a theatre and/or amphitheatre. Another dimension was added to towns when encompassing fortifications were erected. At first usually consisting of no more than an earth bank and a ditch, all were ultimately enclosed by a masonry wall, sometimes with internal towers rising above the top level, and often with monumental gates. In many cases, external towers of varying forms were later added. But even after defences had been built, many towns still had external suburbs, while the amphitheatre was normally left outside the walls for reasons of economy. Minor towns, lacking most of the public buildings of the major counterparts, probably changed less in appearance, the most significant alteration being the slow change from timber construction to masonry or half-timbering; in towns of both types there was probably always a sprinkling of surviving wooden structures. But as with the major towns, many of the lesser examples were provided with protective walls, introducing the same visual alteration in outward appearance.

With the arrival of masonry the colour and texture of both forts and towns will have changed yet again, depending on the type of stone used. In the area south-east of the Chilterns, where there was a lack of good building stone, nodular flint, allied with brick, became the norm; the flint was used raw and unknapped. The normal procedure was to construct a wall of coursed flint, interleaved with bands of brick, which was often used for quoins as well; these courses not only enabled the mason to keep to a level, but also added strength. The exterior surfaces seldom seem to have been rendered, so the outward appearance would have been somewhat rough in texture and of a greyish-white colour, broken up by the smoother red bands and corners of brick. Another method of construction in the same area involved the use of unbaked mud brick, but this would have required plastering, followed by a lime wash; there are occasional instances of colour washes and decorative painting being applied to external surfaces. For more important buildings the flint core of a wall was sometimes encased in a better-quality stone, usually from the series of sandstones and coarse limestones found in the Weald. Thus the theatre at Canterbury was clad in Kentish ragstone, a coarse siliceous limestone, while for finer work still, better-quality stone was brought from further afield: Bath stone, Portland stone, Purbeck marble were all used, and a monumental arch in London was built of Lincolnshire limestone. These different stones would all provide variety in both texture and colour, while the best-quality material would allow the incorporation of architectural features such as colonnades and porticoes, thus enhancing the form.

One oddity within this general area occurs at Colchester. Various horizons in the London clay contain muddy limestones, known locally as septaria. This was used in the form of nodules as a building material in the Roman town; its irregular formation required the use of brick courses as a strengthening material, as with flint. Easily weathered, it imparted a characteristic brownish colour to structures and especially to the town walls, which was in marked contrast to the flint often employed in internal buildings.

Elsewhere in the country, where there was mostly abundant building stone, the visual appearance of forts and towns would be derived from its nature. Thus it might range from the regularly coursed, smooth textured, honey-coloured oolites of the Cotswolds, through the browner shades of the ironstones of Northamptonshire, the whites, greys and pinks of the carboniferous limestones and coarser millstone grits of the Pennines, to the dark brownish-reds of the sandstones of south Wales and parts of the south-west. All were suitable for building, and since local stone was invariably used, all gave their own characteristics to the landscape of which they became part. The only major exception was where use was made of igneous rocks, as in Leicester, where the quarries of Charnwood Forest supplied much building material. The skills to work these rocks had not been developed in Roman times; consequently, they were used as irregular lumps, in much the same way as flint. Finer work was carried out in brick or in millstone grit from the more distant sources in Derbyshire.

As with the towns, so with the rural areas. The villas, farms and country temples would match their urban equivalents, again making use of local materials. Consequently, as today, it would have been possible for any inhabitants of Roman Britain to look at their surroundings and know for a near certainty in which part of the country they were travelling.

2

PRE-ROMAN CHANGES
TO THE LANDSCAPE

As already outlined in the previous chapter, the first clearances of wood and scrub in Britain probably occurred in the Neolithic period with a turn from hunter-gathering to the more settled existence of agriculture and pastoralism. A gradual increase in the population would follow, which, in turn, would lead to a greater demand for more food and hence to more extensive clearances. By the late Bronze Age and early Iron Age, the population had reached considerable numbers, with the concomitant rise in areas under cultivation, and in the growth in number and size of settlements.

At this stage in the development of the countryside, settlements mostly consisted of single farms, probably for extended family groups or small 'villages', with the earliest hilltop enclosures beginning to appear in a number of places. By the time Caesar arrived in Britain hillforts had greatly increased in both number and size, while other settlements had proliferated. Indeed it has been reckoned that most of the land suitable for cultivation or pasture in the area south-east of the Jurassic zone, and possibly in the west Midlands as well, had been cleared; only the thickly forested regions on heavy clay, or the poor, thin acid upland soils, remained.

Although there were numerous variations, the farms and settlements of the later Iron Age all possessed some common characteristic features. Houses were invariably circular, with cone-shaped roofs; occasionally they were surrounded by a low bank and shallow ditch. The size was presumably governed by two factors: the number of inhabitants and the lengths of timbers available for spanning the roof. A single entrance gave access, which was sometimes augmented by a small external porch. In many cases the eaves dropped almost, if not wholly, to ground level, with the circumferential wall being enclosed within the structure. The roofs would have been most frequently covered by thatch, although there is no reason why reeds, bracken, heather or even turf could not have been used in appropriate areas where cereal straw was scarce. The number of houses in any settlement varied greatly from single examples up to dozens, again presumably reflecting the size of the community.

Small square or rectangular structures, usually based on four corner posts, have also been identified alongside the round houses in some settlements; they are usually interpreted as granaries, which were in many cases augmented by storage pits dug in the ground. Simple two-post structures are supposed to have been drying racks for hay or cereals. Most settlements also contained 'working hollows', where it would appear that cooking or cereal-drying took place.

A large number of farms and settlements in the south and east remained un-enclosed, but others were protected by, often at first, a simple palisade. Later in the

Iron Age, a ditch was frequently dug around the outside with the material from it heaped up as an internal or external bank to replace a palisade; it seems likely that some form of fence or hedge was planted on top of the bank. Classic examples are Little Woodbury and Gussage All Saints (Wilts.). A single entrance, normally with a gate, which was sometimes flanked by outwardly extending ditches, provided access to the enclosure. The ditched entrances gave rise on occasion to the so-called 'banjo enclosures' of the southern chalklands. Typical examples of the latter are Bramdean and Owslebury in Hampshire, while the settlement at Tollard Royal on the chalk of Cranborne Chase (Wilts.) is a splendid example of a ditched enclosure.

Elsewhere in the country, the same general arrangements applied, although there were material differences in structure. In the south-west, the enclosures are usually referred to as 'rounds' even though they were often of irregular shape; the outer wall was composed of earth and rubble retained between drystone faces, a method of construction which was often repeated in the walls of the houses, and which is surely the forerunner of the modern Cornish hedge; numerous examples are known. A development unique to this part of the country was the courtyard house, which normally occurs in small groups on the lower moorland slopes, as at Chysauster. Individual houses are roughly oval in outline and constructed, as with the rounds, of earth and rubble banks kept in place by drystone walls. The rooms, up to six in number, were built within the thickness of the outer wall and opened onto a central courtyard, to which a single entrance gave access. They may be seen as a development of the rounds, where each 'house' or 'room' in the latter was absorbed by a massive internal thickening of the perimeter wall; indeed there are instances at Porthmeor and Goldherring of such houses existing inside rounds. Although primarily of pre-Roman date, many rounds continued in use during the Roman period, while the courtyard house is thought to have been a development during that period.

The round finds its counterpart in south-west Wales in the rath, of which Walesland Rath in Pembrokeshire is a prime, excavated example. A number of timber-framed houses, granaries and storage buildings were situated within an oval area bounded by a bank and ditch. In its later stages there was a single entrance, probably surmounted by a gate-tower. Similar basic settlement types, sometimes with minor variations, are to be found in north Wales and the Marches. In the Pennines and north, settlements ranged from a single hut such as West Brandon (Co. Durham) to large agglomerations, amounting in many cases to villages like those at Dalton Parlours (W. Yorks) and Hayhope Knowe in southern Scotland; suitable caves were also occupied.

The essential Iron Age settlement throughout that part of Britain affected by the Roman occupation therefore consisted of one or more round houses, constructed mainly of timber, but in suitable areas also employing drystone walls, and roofed with thatch, reed, bracken, heather or turf; they seldom exceeded 15 m in diameter and most were much smaller, on average about 6 m. Ancillary buildings in the form of square or rectangular storage structures, or granaries, existed in many settlements, but by no means in all. Some were first enclosed by palisades, although banks and ditches later became the norm; others remained open.

It is at this point that the vexed question of protection versus defence arises. Protection would imply no more than a barrier which was effective to keep animals (and children) inside the enclosure, and probably wild animals out. Defence, on the other hand, would imply both an adequate barrier and a platform from which attackers could be repelled. Most of the enclosures, consisting of no more than a palisade or a single bank and ditch, perhaps surmounted by a hedge, which surrounded Iron Age settlements, can be seen as only protective. But when they develop multivallate forms, as in the concentric circle sites in north Wales, something more than just protection seems to be implied, especially where the settlement occupied a hilltop site. From there, no great stretch of the imagination is required to embrace the genuinely defended sites of hillforts, cliff and promontory forts.

As has already been discussed (p. 18) the distribution of this type of fortified enclosure in Britain is very uneven, with over 3,000 known. Rare in the south-east and north, they proliferate in Wessex, the Cotswolds, the Welsh Marches and the south-west. Their construction implies developments in society, with cooperation occuring among individual communities and presumably with the emergence of a dominant leadership. Presumably also, there would be an as yet unquantified association between the size and complexity of a hillfort and the population dependent on it. They also provide evidence for what must have been an endemic form of raiding warfare between rival communities, but whether it is possible to argue from this that the inhabitants of the south-east were more peaceful than those of Wessex or other parts is not easily resolved.

Hillforts and allied structures varied considerably in size, ranging from less than a 1 ha up to nearly 20 ha. Some began as palisaded enclosures, which were converted to univallate structures, which in turn were sometimes developed later to multivallate form; all occupied commanding positions in the local topography. The defences normally consisted of a rampart composed of the upcast of the ditch, perhaps augmented with material quarried from the surface of the interior. In the simplest form this rampart was revetted with timber or a drystone wall at the front, although some were also revetted at the rear. In many instances, more especially where stone or rubble was being employed, horizontal timber strapping has been found in the body of the bank, presumably to provide extra stability by tying the front and rear faces together. The number and form of the gates could also vary considerably; in the simplest a timber-framed gate was placed between terminations of the rampart. More developed examples had the gates set back between inturns of the latter, while the most complex additionally employed an elaborate array of outer banks, ditches and hornworks covering the entrance passages.

Most hillfort interiors were densely occupied with round houses, storage buildings and pits, hay-drying racks and even streets and paths, such as that at the recently excavated Danebury (Hants), although the density tended to vary from site to site and would have depended on many socio-economic factors.

The later Iron Age, more especially in the south-east, saw the growth of a number of valley-side and valley-bottom fortified enclosures, often of considerable size, and defended by massive linear dykes. Not all of the interiors were occupied by buildings and there must have been expanses of woodland, pasture and arable; more than one centre can often be identified.

The appearance of the countryside during the Iron Age will therefore have depended on a number of factors related to the density of settlement, the amount of land cleared for agriculture, the proportions of plough to pasture, the crops grown, and surviving tracts of woodland, scrub, moorland or marsh. Unfortunately, evidence for all this is patchy. It has been claimed that the number of settlements on the southern chalklands numbered thousands, in which case we might infer that little land had been left uncleared. But even here there are considerable variations. For instance, on parts of the South Downs eleven farms or settlements have been identified within an area of 5 km^2, with little more than 0.5 km between some of them. In contrast, on the Marlborough Downs, only three such settlements have been found in the much greater area of nearly 13 km^2 with more than 1.5 km between them. Neither do the North Downs appear to have the same density of settlement as the South Downs. Yet, large open settlements occur frequently on the gravels and flood plain of the upper Thames valley, but with fewer, usually enclosed, situated on the neighbouring Cotswolds to the north.

It has been estimated that there were over 2,000 rounds in the south-west, although not all were necessarily occupied at the same time. In Cornwall alone, calculations show a density of one round to between 2 and 4.5 km^2. In addition there were the villages of courtyard houses as well as unenclosed settlements. Insofar as settlement density is demonstrated, Wales, including the Marches, presents a very similar picture, with the raths, and perhaps rather more enclosed sites. The areas of the upper Severn and Dee valleys seem to have been particularly densely occupied.

The west Midlands, with its tracts of sour, acid soils, presents a somewhat different picture with settlement largely confined to the gravel terraces in river valleys. The remainder would appear to have continued as heavy woodland. Yet, in the east Midlands, settlement was beginning to spread onto the clays as early as the third century BC, suggesting that the lighter soils on gravel had already been occupied to capacity. Also in the east Midlands, settlements surround the Fens, although there is as yet little evidence to show that even the higher parts of the latter were occupied to any great extent, unlike the wetlands of the Somerset levels with their so-called 'lake villages'.

In the Pennines and north, with a much greater variety of soil types, altitudes and micro-climates, understanding of the density of settlement still remains in a highly confused state, with some areas, such as the Yorkshire Wolds, some of the Pennine dales and parts of the north-east having been subjected to detailed surveys, but other parts, including that west of the Pennines, being much less well known. What is becoming clear, though, is that in those areas where detailed surveys have been carried out, the density of settlement is much greater than was once thought, and that the pastoral economy, for so long attributed to the region, was much more mixed, with querns and field systems pointing to a greater degree of cultivation.

Almost all the farms and settlements, of whatever size, detailed above, were connected with field systems, which will have imparted their own characteristic features to the landscape, according to the time of year and the crops being grown. Field boundaries which existed in flat countryside, such as valley bottoms, are seldom visible today, except by aerial survey. But on hill slopes they were usually bounded by lynchets which were mainly formed by the process of ploughing, followed by soil creep downhill. Some lynchets were supplemented by stones and flints taken from the field surfaces and tipped at the edges; they probably supported hedges or fences to keep stock from wandering into growing crops. In areas with suitable stone, drystone walls replaced hedges and fences. Thousands of field systems have been identified in Britain, and many continued in use, sometimes unchanged, sometimes with adaptations, throughout the Roman period, even though their origins lay in the Iron Age or earlier. The size of individual fields varied according to the topography, but they were normally about 0.1–0.2 ha in area, possibly as in the Roman period, representing the amount that one man could plough in a day.

In the earlier Iron Age the principal cereal crop was emmer wheat, coupled to a lesser extent with naked barley; the latter was gradually replaced by the hulled variety. Emmer was not suitable for autumn sowing as it was susceptible to frost; neither was it entirely suitable for heavier soils. Spelt, in contrast, is both hardier and more tolerant and gradually took the place of emmer. Both forms of wheat were bearded so that, when growing, they would have appeared virtually indistinguishable from barley. Small quantities of both rye and oats also seem to have been cultivated, while the Celtic bean made its appearance in the later Iron Age. Not only did the latter provide food for people and fodder for stock, but also, being a nitrogen-fixing legume, improved soil fertility, thus being a useful break crop from the normal cereals. Other crops may have been grown as vegetables or fodder, but were probably more normally harvested from the wild, or as weeds of cultivation such as the valuable Fat Hen. It is important to remember that most crops would have been infested with weeds and would have appeared very different from the pampered cereal fields we see today with their measured fertilizing and herbicidal treatment. Yet this is only a development of the last fifty years or so. Many of the less-vigorous common weed species of cornfields are becoming rare, if not extinct as a result, and the fields which were once (and probably in the Iron Age) scattered with the red of poppies and pheasant's eye, the purple of corncockle, the yellow of charlock, the blue of chicory and cornflower and the golden-centred white flowers of mayweed, are now rarely seen. But in antiquity all would no doubt have contributed to the visual appearance of the countryside in summer. Although weed seeds occur mixed with samples of recovered Iron Age cereals, the quantity is not perhaps as great as might be expected from uncontrolled growth, and we might postulate that hand clearance of weeds was carried out. This is perfectly possible and the present writer, as a schoolboy, remembers well helping to clear ten acres of wheat from an infestation of charlock in the early days of the last war. Not only did weeds compete with the growing crops, but their seeds also contaminated the resulting flour, sometimes imparting a bitter taste.

Apart from the fields described above, other larger areas are often found in the neighbourhood of settlements enclosed by linear ditches and banks. They are sometimes referred to as boundaries of ranches, inside which livestock could be grazed. Smaller enclosures set within them might have been corrals for round-ups. Nor should it be forgotten that cattle, sheep and pigs could be let into fallow, or cultivated fields after the harvest, to fatten on the residue of crop and the weeds, so in turn fertilizing them with manure, and also helping to break up the surface soil; pigs in particular with their habit of rooting in the ground are ideal for this.

An appreciation of a local, contemporary landscape can be obtained by an examination of experimental Iron Age farms created in Hampshire over the last twenty-five years or so. The first was founded on a spur of the South Downs at Butser, near Petersfield, in 1972, although circumstances forced it to move to a new site near Horndean in the early 1990s.

At the centre of the original Butser farm were three round houses, which were modelled on the ground plans of excavated examples. All three provided form from their conical shape, but while two were thatched, the third was clad entirely with turf;

hence there was an immediate variation in colour and texture, ranging from a straw-coloured speckled appearance to bright green blades, with the latter merging into the background scenery, since the turf roots and the grass continues to grow. The fact that such roofs would have needed mowing from time to time is an interesting side-light. If left unmown and raked down in the autumn, a layer of grass thatch would ultimately have accumulated. Adjacent to the houses inside the farmstead enclosure was a series of drying racks, haycocks raised from the ground on timber sub-frames and normally thatched, and storage pits.

The approach to the farmstead, by a wide track leading from the main ridge, was flanked by paddocks for sheep, enclosed with interwoven wattle fencing. In antiquity they would have been used for wintering, lambing, shearing and for annual culls. For much of the year the flocks presumably grazed the neighbouring downland, adding yet another, and this time movable, element to the form and colour of the landscape, but very different from modern flocks since the sheep then bred were much darker in colour, not unlike the Soay, and with the rams at least armed with fearsome curved horns. As with goats, they are capable of climbing and jumping considerable heights and their safe confinement must have caused some problems.

The arable fields were situated beyond the farmstead towards the end of the spur. Here were grown a variety of cereal crops, ranging from the earliest known wheat variety, Einkhorn, to Emmer, Spelt and barley. Since these wheats were bearded, the visual appearance of the fields would have been very similar, the only variation in colour and texture being caused by different rates of growth and maturity. Other plants grown and studied on the experimental farm, either deliberately or by accident, were the Celtic bean, flax and Fat Hen, as well as other weeds of cultivation.

The flanks of the spur on which the farmstead stood were covered in light woodland. Whether or not they were so in antiquity is not known, but, had they been, coppicing might have played its part, producing hazel rods for fencing, baskets and building, and more mature timber for heavier construction work.

Although there were variations in colour and texture caused by differences in the materials of construction, one Iron Age farmstead would therefore have looked very like any other, no matter in what part of the country it was found, with the conical roofs of the houses providing most of the form.

There can be little doubt, though, that the greatest impact on the countryside's appearance was provided by the hillforts and other defended enclosures. Their normally commanding positions would have made them visible for many kilometres, more so if constructed on chalk, with the glaring white of the newly excavated rock shining like a beacon to proclaim their positions. Time would have moderated the effect with the growth of grass, weeds, moss and algae, only for the chalk to be re-exposed if the ditches were cleaned or recut and the banks supplemented. Texture and colour was also provided by the nature of any revetments used to retain the ramparts, whether of timber or stone, or a combination of both.

The last aspect of Iron Age Britain which would have made a visual impact on the countryside is the extensive system of trackways. Many of these can still be seen as they approach settlements through field systems, but there were also long-distance tracks which traversed south-eastern England. The known examples all keep to high ground along the chalk or oolite escarpments. The Harroway starts near the eastern edge of Salisbury Plain and ultimately runs along the top of the southern scarp of the

North Downs as far as Folkestone. In the middle ages much of its length was used as a pilgrim track to Canterbury and can still be followed today. The Icknield Way also begins in the vicinity of Salisbury Plain and thence runs by way of the Marlborough Downs and the scarp of the Chilterns to the Norfolk coast, skirting the Fens to end apparently near the entrance to the Wash; there was a continuation along the Lincolnshire Wolds on the other side of the Wash up to the Humber, later perpetuated by a Roman equivalent road. The third main route, the Jurassic Way, used the oolites of the Cotswolds and Northamptonshire, starting from the region around Bath and then meandering along the higher ground as far as the Humber. It is possible that both these last two routes continued into Yorkshire, although there is no surviving evidence for them north of the Humber. No doubt other long-distance routes also existed, and it has been suggested that the Whiteway leading north from Cirencester has a prehistoric origin; its ultimate destination may have been south Wales or the upper Severn valley.

But as mentioned earlier (p. 20), these trackways probably only had a minor visual effect on the landscape. At the worst, they were probably no more than muddy lanes, at the best grass-covered, according to the time of year and traffic density; wear might have created hollows in places, so that they were flanked by banks on which scrub or grass, accompanied by a natural flora of mainly lime-loving plants, would grow. In other places they undoubtedly penetrated woodland. But their adherence mainly to the natural contours would have made them all but invisible from a distance, but for the people and animals moving along them.

This then was the landscape which the Roman army found when it arrived in Britain, first under Caesar, then under Claudius, and which it inherited from the Iron Age in Britain.

3

ROMAN ARRIVAL

The army and the landscape

Caesar's arrival in Britain, first in 55 BC, then in 54, made very little difference to the landscape, so little in fact that none of the camps or other fortifications, which he must have constructed, are known today even by aerial photography: as far as the landscape is concerned, Caesar never came to Britain!

The invasion by Claudius, in contrast, was a very different matter. It set in train events which were to last about 350 years, and which had a major impact on the countryside of England, Wales and a large part of Scotland and left lasting features, some of which are still visible today.

Since the invasion force landed in the south-east, primarily at Richborough, the first alterations took place in that part of the country with the construction of campaign camps and presumably some more permanent fortifications. So began the gradual deforestation of the surviving areas of woodland, to provide timber for the increasing amount of construction work. Unfortunately there is little evidence for the army's march through Kent to the Thames. A fortified beach-head has been identified at Richborough, although it was not large enough to have accommodated the entire force. A fort is known within the Iron Age oppidum at Canterbury, another near Faversham and very probably another in the London region. Otherwise there is nothing to show for the advance until Colchester was reached, where an auxiliary fort and legionary fortress were established. But the line of the advance must have been marked by at least a cleared strip of land, probably with bridges over the rivers Stour, Medway and Thames, which ultimately became the road known as Watling Street.

Colchester therefore saw the construction of the first known legionary fortress, as well as an auxiliary fort, in Britain. It is more than likely that the oppidum of Camulodumum contained at least two centres, one in the Gosbecks area at Stanway and another, somewhat later, at Sheepen. The present writer long ago suggested that they represented the tribal capitals of the Trinovantes and the Catuvellauni respectively, the latter having conquered and subsumed the former *c.* AD 10. It is not surprising, therefore, that the legionary fortress was constructed close to the main centre of resistence at Sheepen, while the more friendly Trinovantes were given the protection of an auxiliary fort.

But before work could start on the fortress, a temporary camp was established just inside the western edge of the oppidum's defences. Bounded on the western side by a triple dyke, it would have provided tented accommodation for the troops. The brown leather tents would have merged into the background of plough and pasture and had little visual impart on the scenery, although no doubt they were embellished by the coloured standards of the legion and its cohorts. The fortress, though, was another matter, constructed on a gravel spur towards the north-eastern side of the oppidum and immediately above a sharp drop to the valley of the river Colne.

From the outside, the principal eye-catching focus of the fortress would have been its rectangular shape, surrounded by ramparts, set with gate-towers, and possibly interval-towers which probably rose to perhaps twice the height of the former. The rampart, up to 3–4 m high, would at this stage of the conquest have been constructed of material derived from digging the ditch in front of it, retained between cheeks made of blocks of clayey turf. The blocks were cut to a standard width and thickness so that they could be laid in regular courses. When first constructed, therefore, they would have appeared as wide brown lines probably interspersed with thinner bands of green; but gradually the grass at the surface would have grown and covered all with a uniform green or brown, according to the time of year. A regular fatigue duty in the summer must have been mowing this grass on the rampart faces. The ditches were also usually kept clean of silt and weeds, so revealing bare gravel surfaces for most of the time. Parts of an experimental fort built at Baginton near Coventry in 1966–73 demonstrated the required frequency of both these operations, but it was interesting that the growth of grass on the rampart faces was very uneven, while that on the sides of the ditch was very slow. The rampart would also have been topped with a crenellated timber breastwork, most likely of horizontal wattles woven between uprights, although there is a little evidence to show that close boarding may have been used on some occasions; both would provide variations of colour and texture, according to the nature of the wood used.

The internal buildings of the fortress, such as barracks, were mostly of a single storey, so that little more than roofs would have shown above the rampart. The nature of the roofing material is uncertain, but if tiles had been used, then red would have topped the green and brown of the ramparts. Some buildings, however, were higher than the barracks; the basilica at the back of the principia was a large aisled hall which would have risen to about twice the height of its surrounding structures. The granaries, with their raised floors, would also have been somewhat higher.

The external walls of the buildings in the fortress were constructed of clay blocks set on timber beams lying on top of low masonry plinths. The outside surfaces were probably lime-washed for protection against the weather, so that below the red of the roofs, white would have been the prominent colour, until dirt, moss and algae dimmed the brightness. This method of construction was largely peculiar to Colchester. Elsewhere in the same period most military installations were built of wattle-and-daub on timber frames, although, given a coating of lime, the external appearance would have been very similar. The auxiliary fort at Stanway would almost certainly have been constructed in this manner, but excavation has yet to confirm it. Consequently the overall appearance would have matched the fortress but on a reduced scale.

It is to be assumed that both fortress and fort occupied pasture or arable land within the oppidum. A considerable area of neighbouring woodland was no doubt cleared to provide the large quantity of timber needed in the construction work (p. 19); this, in turn, would have provided additional areas for agriculture, augmenting the existing production of cereals so as to feed an extra 6,000–7,000 men, as well as providing fodder and grazing for numerous horses. In addition, quarries were dug for clay and aggregates, while the Sheepen part of the oppidum was soon converted into a works depot for the production of brick, tile and metalwork and later pottery, consuming prodigious quantities of fuel, and presumably covered for much of the time by a pall of smoke. Situated almost due west of the fortress and in the line of the prevailing winds, the latter must have been something of an irritation to the garrison. It can be seen, therefore, that a marked change must have occurred in the local landscape.

The ensuing advance of the Roman army followed three main lines: one almost due north in the direction of Lincoln, the second north-west into the west Midlands and the third south-west towards Wiltshire and Dorset. Each was headed by a legion with accompanying auxiliary forces. These lines of advance were presumably first marked by wide strips of cleared land, later to be perpetuated by three main roads: Ermine Street, Watling Street and the Portway. Striking across the contours in a series of straight lines, their impact on the landscape must have been far greater than any corresponding Iron Age trackways. Moreover, when the metalled roads were constructed, the countryside along them was further scarred by quarries and pits for aggregate, although these would fill and grow over in time.

We know little of the battles and skirmishes fought during these advances and even less of the battlegrounds, except where they impinged on hillforts such as Maiden Castle and Hod Hill. Even then the effects can only be seen in excavations and no surface traces survive in the form of siege works. The advances would also have been accompanied by a series of campaign camps, but none have so far been identified.

The initial advance was halted roughly on a line running from the Severn estuary to the Humber, which was eventually marked by the cross-country road known as the Foss Way. This road is one of the more remarkable examples of Roman surveying practice. Between Lincoln and Seaton in Devon, a distance of nearly 400 km, it never deviates more than 10 km either side of a straight line joining the two terminals, and represents a great swathe cutting across the countryside from north-east to south-west. Its track has been perpetuated by many kilometres of modern road, which in places still ride the raised agger of the Roman forerunner, as indeed do parts of Ermine Street, Watling Street and the Portway. Consequently, it must be concluded that these roads survived long after the Roman period (p. 121), many lengths also being adopted as parish boundaries, and thus have become permanent features in the modern landscape.

Once the main advance had ceased, a series of fortresses and forts was built in the forward area. This would have resulted in considerably more woodland clearance for timber and also probably the requisitioning of Iron Age pasture or cultivation, since many of the selected sites lay close to existing settlements. Most were placed in valley bottoms and a favourite position was a raised, level terrace adjacent to a river, such as the vexillation fortress at Longthorpe, near Peterborough, the first legionary fortress at Gloucester and the auxiliary forts at Cirencester and Dorchester (Oxon.). Notable exceptions were the auxiliary forts situated inside existing Iron Age hillforts such as those at Hod Hill (Dorset), South Cadbury (Somerset) and Hembury (Devon). The legionary fortress at Lincoln, although built a decade or so after the invasion, was likewise placed on the high ground above Lincoln edge, overlooking the valley of the river Witham, which here cuts through the Jurassic ridge from west to east (fig. 12). Consequently, whereas those forts situated in river valleys would only have been visible from the surrounding higher ground, the hilltop sites, as with the Iron Age hillforts that some replaced, would have been seen from a much greater distance, thus exerting more influence on the landscape.

Figure 12 Lincoln Edge from the west. The cathedral (arrowed) stands just south-east of the site of the legionary principia.

A Roman fort was a Roman fort and all would have appeared similar in form at this stage of the conquest, since the materials of construction – timber, turf, wattle-and-daub – were the same for all. Only perhaps in the roofs was there any variation, since thatch or shingles might have replaced tiles, so providing a diversity of colour and texture. A certain amount of land surrounding a fort would have been requisitioned to provide pasture for horses. Some of it might have been derived from woodland clearance during the construction work, but the total amount would depend on the nature of the garrison. A quingenary ala of cavalry required some 360 ha of pasture for its horses, but the area would be diminished for a part-mounted cohort and again for an infantry regiment. Presumably this pasture was situated as close to the fort as possible, so that we can imagine a stretch of land at least 3.6 km long and 1 km wide being taken over in the valley of the river Churn for the cavalry regiment stationed at Cirencester. Moreover, the horses of this same regiment consumed as much as 1,000 tonnes of hay, plus hard feed, a year. About another 150 tonnes of cereals can be added for the trooper's annual rations. It is difficult to postulate yields of Iron Age cereal crops, although experiments have shown that an average of 1–2 tonnes per hectare is not unrealistic. Consequently, approximately 75–150 ha of cultivated land was needed to provide basic rations. Corresponding hay yields have not yet been assessed, but to provide in excess of 1,000 tonnes would have earmarked yet another appreciable area. This hay and the necessary cereals were normally provided by the local communities, either as a direct tax, usually at a rate of about 10 per cent of production, or at a controlled price, either of which must have been a considerable burden, particularly at first. In reality, therefore, the figure of 75–100 ha quoted above would be equivalent in total to 750–1,000 ha, or

7.5–10 km^2 of cultivated land, if a 10 per cent exaction was enforced. As time passed, however, production was no doubt increased by more land clearance. So the arrival of an auxiliary regiment in a district cannot but have caused a considerable impact on the appearance of the countryside.

It is normally argued that the placing of forts was governed only by strategic and tactical requirements. But there may have been an additional consideration, if these figures are taken into account: something in excess of 10–20 km^2 was required to service each one. The distance between forts could therefore have been influenced by this need, providing the other two factors were also met.

The following decades saw the army advance into south and central Wales, with the further construction of campaign camps, forts and fortresses, and roads. The overall effect on the countryside will have been similar to that already observed in the Midlands and south-east, with deforestation for timber supplies, requisitioning of land, followed probably by a gradual increase in cultivation. In the hilly country of Wales, most of this activity took place in the river valleys, the hilltops being little touched except for the possible temporary interruption of a campaign camp. Here many of the latter are still visible on the surface as low mounds and depresssions on the lines of, respectively, banks and ditches, although the activity was short-lived and the sites would soon have grown over with natural vegetation once occupation had ceased; it may though at first have been of a coarser nature due to the disturbance of the subsoil and the digging of such things as rubbish and latrine pits.

The only exceptions to the 'timber-and-turf' appearances of these forts and fortresses were the masonry bath-houses. These were normally placed outside the ramparts for auxiliary forts, but inside the fortresses, such as Exeter. Built usually of local stone, but often augmented with brick, with tile roofs, and often higher than surrounding structures, they would have been more visible from a distance and so provided a greater impact on the form, texture and colour of the local countryside.

The Boudiccan rebellion only affected the south-eastern landscape of Britain, primarily in the new urban centres (p. 56). A decade of ensuing if uneasy peace was followed by further advances into north Wales, northern England and Scotland, so extending the 'military landscape' to many new areas. But the forts and fortresses were still being built of the same materials, so the visual appearance was much the same as before. Only at Inchtuthil, a legionary fortress built on the banks of the river Tay in Scotland, can the start of a significant change be observed. Here the fortress was ultimately surrounded by a stone wall placed in front of the rampart. It was constructed of local, reddish-pink conglomeratic sandstone which was quarried from Gourdie Hill, some 3 km north of the fortress. It has been calculated that up to 38,000 m^3 of rock was removed from this quarry, leaving a massive scar on the landscape, which can still be seen today, although only about 15,000 m^3 was used for the wall; the remainder must have been waste. When freshly built, therefore, the reddish-pink-coloured wall of the fortress will have been in marked contrast to the original green and brown of the turf and timber rampart, although no doubt it soon weathered to a darker colour. Somewhat surprisingly the timber gates were not rebuilt in stone, so creating another contrast between them and the wall. Apart from the fortress and the quarries, the countryside around was further disturbed by a number of temporary camps, used by the garrison during construction work, and by a compound containing a masonry bath-house.

The quantity of timber required to build the fortress has already been mentioned in Chapter 1, and is equivalent to nearly $20\,\mathrm{km^2}$ of clear-felled woodland. Unfortunately, there is no evidence to show the state of the land around Inchtuthil before the Roman arrival. The area occupied by the fortress and its associated camps and other works probably does not exceed more than $2\,\mathrm{km^2}$. Even if this area had been fully forested, total clearance would have provided only about one-tenth of the requirements. Moreover, the species of trees present, most likely conifers, birch and poor-quality oak, were not always adequate for the main structural timbers of the fortress defences and buildings, although they would have been suitable for lesser purposes. It is more than probable, therefore, that the bulk of the main timbers were brought up from the south, perhaps even from accumulated stockpiles in the Midlands (p. 19), and were already partly prefabricated. Nevertheless, provision of the lesser building members, such as the infilling of walls, and possibly shingles for the roofs, and not forgetting also the need for prodigious quantities of fuel, would have lead rapidly to wholesale clearance of surrounding woodlands for a considerable distance from the fortress. But much of the area that we might envisage as having been cleared would, unless kept that way, have partly regenerated as scrub or coppice by the time the fortress was abandoned *c.* 86.

Seen from a distance, therefore, perhaps from the hills to the north, the fortress would have been situated in a large cleared area, probably covered in scrub or coarse pasture, on the north bank of the river Tay. Rising above the pink sandstone walls were the four timber gate-towers, with the whole surrounded by a wide and deep ditch, interrupted by causeways at the gates. The principal buildings could be distinguished rising above rampart level, and possibly roofed with red tiles. The barracks and many of the other buildings would have been tucked down at rampart level and, although some may have had tile roofs, most were probably of shingles or perhaps even thatch – overall patches of red intermingled with yellow, brown or grey, and each with the appropriate texture. Where walls were visible, they would be starkly white from lime-wash. There is slight evidence for window glass, which when caught by the sun would flash its distinctive message across the country. Nevertheless, in the centre was a large gap, for the praetorium was never built, and was left as a levelled area next to the principia. Another fort at Fendoch, on the edge of the Highlands, demonstrates the way in which a signal tower could be used to enhance vision. The fort was established on a slight plateau near the mouth of Glenalmond, which at that point is called the Sma' Glen. But the view up the Sma' Glen from the fort was restricted, so a signal tower was built to act as its eyes, looking both forward up the glen (fig. 13) and backward to the fort (fig. 14).

The first Roman advance into Scotland only lasted for some twenty to thirty years at the most, after which there came a controlled withdrawal ultimately to the Tyne–Solway isthmus. But during the withdrawal a temporary frontier may have been established along the Gask Ridge in Perthshire. This ridge of sandstone lies east–west, north of the river Earn, and carried the main Roman road to the north; along its length was erected a series of timber watch-towers, each with wide views to front and rear. Whatever the original vegetation had been, most must have been cleared to provide the field of vision. Set in heather-clad moorland, rising to a height of some $10\,\mathrm{m}$ and surrounded by a rampart and ditch, the towers would have dominated the horizon from whichever aspect they were seen.

Figure 13 View up the Sma' Glen from the Fendoch signal station.

The early second century also saw the extension of a significant change, first observed at Inchtuthil (p. 34), in the visual appearance of forts and fortresses. This was caused by the increasing use of stone in the defences and internal buildings, beginning first at the three main fortresses at York, Chester and Caerleon. At York, three types of stone were available: millstone grit from the Pennines, Magnesian limestone from near Tadcaster, and Jurassic limestone, either from the North Yorkshire moors, or from just north of Brough-on-Humber. Each of these materials has its own distinct characteristics. Millstone grit occurs in large, coarsely-grained, pinkish-brown blocks which were suitable for monumental structures. Magnesian limestone is normally fine-grained, greyish-white in colour, sometimes with a pink tinge, and was mostly used in small block-work, as in the defences, although larger pieces are also found. The Jurassic oolites were an attractive yellowy-golden-brown, also with a fine grain; since it easily laminated it made excellent roofing slates and was so used in conjunction with tiles. There was, though, a tendency for freshly exposed surfaces to darken in time to a greyish colour. Consequently, the use of these materials gave the fortress a variety of colours and textures, dominated by the walls, gates, interval-towers and principal internal buildings, and supplemented by the red of tile roofs and the white or colour of plastered walls.

Both legionary fortresses at Chester and Caerleon were more fortunate in having local supplies of sandstone ready to hand; indeed Chester is built on a sandstone plateau overlooking the river Dee. Here the stone, as at Caerleon, was mostly dark red in colour, although it also contained veins of yellow-grey, micaceous material, which laminated easily and so was suitable for roofing-slates. Small quantities of 'pudding stone', a quartz-pebble conglomerate, were also used at Caerleon, mostly in the rough for buried features such as foundations. Consequently, the visual

Figure 14 The fort at Fendoch (Perthshire) seen from its outlying signal station. It occupies the slightly raised plateau at the base of the far hills.

appearances of both fortresses will have been similar and more uniform in colour than York.

It must also be remembered that large clearances accompanied all three fortresses, dating back to the original timber structures, and resembling those at Inchtuthil (p. 35). But in these instances, much of the land so cleared would have been maintained for agricultural use to provide the grazing, fodder and food for the human and animal inhabitants. Nevertheless, it is more than probable that some was kept as regenerated woodland, which, by periodical coppicing, provided fuel for the fortresses' many requirements.

The withdrawal from Scotland was eventually checked on the Tyne–Solway isthmus, and there was built the first permanent frontier of Britain. This is not the place to discuss its strategic or tactical merits; arguments still continue and no doubt will do so in the future. That aside, as with many things Roman, there is a certain ruthlessness attached to Hadrian's Wall, striding as it does across hill and valley alike. The effect, no doubt intended, was, and still is, intimidating. A massive stone wall about 5 m high, topped with merlons to add at least another 2 m, punctuated at frequent intervals by turrets and gate-towers of about double the height, and often occupying an eminent position in the landscape, such as along the Whin Sill in the central section, can have been nothing but intimidating. The stone normally used for the wall-facings was a hard quartzose grit, and numerous quarries from which it was extracted have been identified along the Wall. The facing stones were cut almost to a standard size, mostly with a smooth finish, although sometimes broached. Consequently, the textural appearance was very regular, and only varied by the larger blocks used in the gates of forts and milecastles; the colour was also uniform, being a light grey, sometimes with a pale pinkish tinge, which would stand out strongly from the generally green or brown background of grass and trees.

But at the start the desired effect of intimidation was somewhat vitiated by a change in plan which caused different materials to be used westward from the river Irthing. The reasons for this change have also been much discussed without any firm conclusions being reached. This stretch, which extended to the terminal point at Bowness-on-Solway, was built entirely of turf, with presumably a timber breastwork: just over 6 m wide at the base, it probably stood to a height of some 4 m. The milecastles here were similarly constructed with turf ramparts and timber-framed gates and buildings within, but the turrets were built of masonry from the first. The overall appearance, therefore, would have seen the turrets of pale grey stone standing out from the generally more muted wall and ramparts, which would blend better with the surroundings.

A less prominent feature, only properly visible at close quarters, was the great ditch which fronted the Wall along its entire length, but for an interruption near Limestone Corner where it passes across a ridge of very hard dolomite. Presumably the ditch was kept free of grass, weeds and scrub, which would have grown slowly after its excavation. Adding to the cleared effect on the landscape was the area behind the Wall which contained the garrison forts and which was ultimately bounded to the south by the Vallum. The latter consisted of a broad ditch flanked on both sides by turf-revetted mounds which were set back some 10 m from the corresponding lips, the whole being *c.* 40 m across. Where access was required to forts, causeways were first constructed across it to communicate with the Stanegate, an earlier road running behind the Vallum at least from Corbridge westwards. This road was finally replaced by the Military Way which connected all forts and milecastles together but only after the Vallum had ceased to function. Many other changes were incorporated in this defensive system, the most important being the replacement of the turf wall by masonry, although of narrower gauge.

When taken altogether, the Wall, the Vallum, the forts, roads, the scars left by quarries, the forts to the rear and the outpost forts beyond must have brought about startling changes to the landscape in a broad sweep from the mouth of the Tyne right across to the Solway Firth and then continuing to a lesser degree down the Cumbrian coast as far as Moricambe Bay.

Unfortunately, all too little attention has been paid to environmental evidence from excavations on the Wall and its related structures. There are suggestions from Corbridge that land was being cleared and cultivated during the prehistoric period; pre-Roman tree-root systems were also uncovered, and it has been suggested that scrub covered the site immediately before the first Roman occupation.

Rather more evidence has been derived from Chesterholm, where it was shown that large quantities of bracken, presumably harvested from near the fort, were used as a floor covering. The survival of much wood in the wet deposits showed that birch, oak, hazel and ash were the commonest species being used, although there was also rowan, yew, pine and cherry; birch appears to have been the principal building material, showing that unseasoned local supplies were garnered, in contrast to the suggestions made about Inchtuthil (p. 35), although these trees are unlikely to have provided large structural members. Gorse and heather were also represented, while walnuts were no doubt an import. The remarkable collection of wooden writing tablets from this fort also provide useful snippets of information. References to oxherds and swineherds imply the presence of both pasture and woodland, while purchase of barley and other cereals in large quantities – presumably from near at hand – would suggest cultivation on some scale in the vicinity.

The construction of the new frontier, following the first withdrawal from Scotland, also led to the abandonment of some forts in Wales and northern England, more especially those east of the Pennines. It is usually assumed that forts which were evacuated were also dismantled; this was certainly the case in Scotland, where the buildings at Inchtuthil, at Fendoch at the southern end of the Sma' Glen and at Strageath on the river Earn were systematically demolished. All provided some evidence for the recovery of major timbers, presumably for use elsewhere, while smaller debris was usually burnt on site. Apart from the buildings, ramparts were normally slighted into ditches, and at Inchtuthil the curtain wall was thrown down. Nothing was left which could have been of any possible use to an enemy, and it would not have been long before nature again took over, covering the sites with weeds, grass and ultimately scrub and trees. Probably the only sign that they had once been occupied would have been prodigious growths of nettles, always one of the first weeds to re-establish itself on disturbed land rich in phosphates from human and animal excreta. It is interesting that a soil sample taken from a layer deep in the excavations at Cirencester, and uncontaminated by modern seeds, when submitted to germination tests, produced a fine crop of nettles and nothing else (p. 74), demonstrating not only the longevity of the seeds, but also the commonest species to occur on waste, previously-occupied ground. When a fort was reoccupied, as they often were, swathes of nettles would have been one of the surest indicators of the position of the earlier one. Even now they can point to the sites of earlier habitations and farm buildings, although nothing else remains.

The construction of the new frontier led to a consolidation of the 'military' landscape in much of Wales, northern England and southern Scotland. In service terms, each fort or fortress required a considerable area around it to provide food, fodder, pasture and fuel, in addition to any periodical demands for the materials of construction such as stone, timber and aggregates, which may have come from farther afield. Much of this was probably provided by local communities living in the area, although there is some evidence that by the later second century, members of the garrison were also engaged in farming. Under Hadrian there was something in excess of seventy occupied auxiliary forts in Britain of various sizes and types; most were occupied by infantry, perhaps as much as three-quarters, with about one-fifth by cavalry and the remainder (one-tenth) made up of part-mounted regiments; then there were the three legionary fortresses also to take into account. Working on the figures given on p. 19 above, a very rough estimate would indicate that an area of between 1,000 and 2,000 km^2, roughly the size of Kent, would have been needed to provide these military installations with their basic supplies. These figures can only be a very broad approximation, and are probably an under-estimate, since so many factors enter into the calculation, such as crop yields, which would depend on the type of soil and weather, but they serve to give some idea of the scale of land clearance which the army alone in Britain required. Admittedly we do not know how much had already been cleared; such evidence as there is suggests quite a large proportion, but even allowing for this the effect on the landscape would have been profound.

The Roman army's return to Scotland in 140 led to further changes with the construction of a new frontier, the Antonine Wall. The visual contrast of this work with Hadrian's Wall was considerable, since, apart from a minority of forts and some internal buildings such as granaries and bath-houses, the curtain, the other fort ramparts and internal buildings were built of turf and timber, so blending far better with the countryside. Nevertheless, when coupled with the Military Way, which ran some 35–45 m to the rear of the Wall and the ditch in front, it represented a cleared strip of ground of some width extending from Bridgeness on the Forth to Old Kilpatrick on the Clyde. As with Hadrian's Wall, the central section crossed high ground, at one point of which a short stretch of the ditch was never dug owing to the hardness of the rock (fig. 15).

Coupled with the new Wall and its installations, a number of outpost forts were constructed along the old Flavian road leading north, notably at Ardoch, Strageath and Bertha, where the earlier sites of the Agricolan forts were quickly identified – no doubt helped by the nettles – and reconstructed, although to different plans. Much of lowland Scotland was also reoccupied, again reusing earlier sites, while Hadrian's Wall was reduced to little more than a care and maintenance state. But apart from clearing young growth of scrub, saplings and general undergrowth, it is doubtful if any other major alteration took place in the landscape, outside the line of the new Wall, which had not already been effected earlier under Agricola.

The new advance into Scotland did not last long. A temporary withdrawal in the 150s was accompanied by the reoccupation of some forts in northern England and in Wales, but the Antonine Wall as a frontier seems finally to have been abandoned in the early 180s, when Hadrian's Wall, together with its outpost forts, once more became the boundary of the province and continued so until the end of the fourth century. The Severan campaigns into Scotland in the early third century can have had little effect on the countryside, apart from the areas cleared for campaign camps. Consequently, from now on a state of equilibrium probably existed in the military landscapes of Wales and the north, although it is likely that increasing areas were converted to rough pasture and cultivation. In this respect the field systems around the fort at Housesteads are of interest. On the hillsides south and east of the fort are visible terraces, which, while they may be of pre-Roman origin, were almost certainly worked in the Roman period; overlying them are traces of medieval and later fields. It is difficult to tell, though, whether they were primarily connected with the fort, or with the large vicus that grew to its peak in the third and fourth centuries.

Probably one of the chief causes of further clearance of woodland was to provide the huge quantities of fuel required for domestic and industrial purposes, with the army heavily involved in the latter and, in this context, with military bath-houses consuming the lion's share of the former. These implications are dealt with more fully later (p. 96).

From the foregoing sections it will be seen that much of the long term 'military' landscape was situated mostly in Wales, northern England and Scotland. But in the third century this was to change, with new threats to the south and east coasts. Along these shores was built a chain of massive masonry forts, unlike anything seen previously in Britain: the forts of the Saxon Shore. They were sited adjacent to natural harbours and contained naval units as well as the military garrisons. They also represented a change in strategy, whereby the forts became defended strong-points which could protect, not only the garrison, but also important stores.

The earliest forts in this chain were constructed at Brancaster, just east of the mouth of the Wash, and Reculver, on the north Kent shore near the entrance to the Wantsum.

Figure 15 Unexcavated ditch of the Antonine Wall, east of Croy Hill.

Both were larger than normal auxiliary forts, with more substantial walls, *c.* 3 m thick, backed by ramparts. There were internal angle-towers at Brancaster but not at Reculver. The walls of both were faced with small flint, but with ironstone and chalk mixed in at Brancaster. Judging from the height of the surviving wall at Pevensey, they could have been anything up to 8 m high, topped with a parapet, merlons and embrasures, and with gate-towers and, at Brancaster, angle-towers, rising perhaps as much again above the wall. Larger sandstone blocks were used to form jambs and arches. The height of the walls would have precluded all but the major buildings from being seen from outside the fort. The external visual appearance would, therefore, have been made up of the regular texture formed by the small blockwork of the facings and varying in colour from the greyish-green of sandstone to the brown of ironstone. Above this level might have appeared the red, probably tiled, roof of the principia. Brancaster was surrounded by a single ditch, Reculver by two, which however were allowed to silt soon after the fort was built, and presumably, therefore, were soon covered by grass and weeds. Apart from the principal buildings, most of the structures inside these forts appear to have been of timber and so would have resembled, in appearance, forts of the first century, with lime-washed walls and red tile roofs.

By the end of the third century, other forts had been added to the chain, the most notable perhaps being Richborough, not only for its present state of preservation, but also for the extensive excavations carried out in the 1930s. It had one further distinguishing feature. As the main site of the army's landing in 43, it became also the place where a great monument was erected to mark the gateway to Britain, probably begun by Domitian to commemorate the conquest of the island, which had culminated in the campaigns of Agricola. It consisted of a *quadrifons*, or a four-way arch, which stood to a height of about 26 m and was almost certainly topped with a group of

Figure 16 Patterned stonework in the north wall of the Saxon Shore fort at Richborough (Kent).

statuary, perhaps adding another 5–10 m to the height. It was faced throughout with white Carrara marble from Italy, although some Pentelic marble from Greece was also found in the excavations; the latter has a distinctive sparkle on a pure white ground. Several inscriptions were cut in the marble, while others were made up of bronze letters; both bronze and marble statuary were included, providing colour contrasts. With its height and brilliant white colour, glaring with the sun on it, it would have been visible for kilometres around, and for a considerable distance out to sea. The cooling towers of the present Richborough power station, although much higher, stand up well when seen from the hills above Canterbury, and it is not improbable that the monument was visible from the same place, a distance of nearly 25 km. It will also have aided navigation for any ships sailing from the Gaulish coast.

But by the end of the third century it was probably in a state of disrepair, so much so that it was dismantled when the masonry Saxon Shore fort was built and the site turned probably into the principia. Much of the marble was burnt for lime in the construction work, while larger blocks of sandstone from the core were reused, more especially at the west gate. As with many of the later Saxon Shore forts, the walls, 3.3 m thick, were relieved by double tile bonding courses at about 1 m intervals. The exterior facing in small greensand ashlars was interspersed by blocks of brown ironstone and creamy-white limestone, which in one place were incorporated in a regular pattern (fig. 16). This use of contrasting stones to create a variegated effect can be seen more completely applied in the third-century walls of Le Mans in northern Gaul, and in an external tower at Cologne. The intention was clearly meant to be decorative, so as to relieve an otherwise uniformly textured and coloured expanse of masonry, thus making a statement about both the masons employed on the work and also the originators of the scheme. In all the later forts of this series, the great expanse of blank wall was further relieved by external towers, rising well above the parapets. These varied in form, from semi-circular, U-shaped, horseshoe-shaped to rectangular and were usually constructed in the same manner as the curtain walls. Neither were all these forts regular in plan, as at Richborough. Dover and Lympne appear to have been irregular polygons, while Pevensey is vaguely egg-shaped.

The west coast was also provided with similar coastal forts, although they did not form part of a systematic chain. Cardiff is the best known and also the most typical, with its massive walls, in which, though, slabs of granite replaced tiles as the bonding courses. The chief difference lies in the external towers, which were pentagonal in form.

The last military work to effect the landscape was restricted to the Yorkshire, and possibly Durham, coast-lines. There was built in the late fourth century a sequence of signal stations. Each station was situated on high ground, such as the cliffs at Scarborough, and consisted of a central tower set in a small squarish courtyard and surrounded by a wall with towers at the rounded angles. It has been estimated that the height of the central tower was about 21 m, and the perimeter wall 15 m. Situated on the skyline, overlooking dramatic cliffs and with mostly open moorland behind, they must have been visible for many kilometres and exerted a considerable impact on the coastal scenery.

The final stage of the military landscape in Britain was abandonment, when the army formally withdrew from the province. Even then a residual civilian occupation occasionally lingered on in some forts, but not for any length of time, and the return to nature was seldom long delayed.

4

PLOUGH AND PASTURE

Agents for change

The first clearances of natural vegetation for agricultural purposes must have been laborious affairs, with only the most primitive tools, even after fire had done its work. Land which has been accidentally burned, or deliberately swaled, rapidly regenerates and within two or three years it is often hard to see where the burning took place; seeds which escaped the flames soon germinate in the newly enriched soil, while others come in from the surroundings on the wind or in bird droppings. Consequently, it must have been a continuous fight to prevent crops from being swamped by this new growth, and it can be done only by repeated hoeing or manual weeding. Clearance of woodland increased the problem with tree roots to be dug out. Nowadays, fearsome machines with giant, wide-bladed circular saws soon reduce even the most stubborn tree stumps to chips, but before they were invented, only axes and mattocks could be used in a tedious and time-consuming job; admittedly, animal power could be employed to drag the stumps out of the ground once the main roots had been severed. It is hardly surprising, therefore, that it is usually assumed that widespread forest clearance did not begin until the Iron Age, when iron tools were introduced. This process was rapidly accelerated during the Roman period, not because the Roman implements were much better in quality, but tempering of the forged iron produced improved cutting edges, and there were simply far more of them.

Clearance of scrub or woodland required cutting implements of which a number were available in the Roman period. The felling axe was of greatest importance and a typical example from the fort at Newstead measured 25 cm in length with a blade 11 cm wide. Such an axe, weighing nearly 3 kg would have been capable of cutting through most mature timber. A wide variety of small axes, billhooks and slashers (long-handled billhooks) were available for cleaning the trunk of a large tree, or for clearing saplings and undergrowth. What has yet to be determined is precisely how a large tree-trunk was cut into standards. Saws of two main types are known. Straight, single-handed forms were mostly small and were used primarily for carpentry and pruning. Bow- or frame-saws were also in use and could be larger in size, but whether they were adequate for cutting longitudinally along the trunk of a hardwood tree seems doubtful. To do so effectively requires a saw pit with a long, two-handed saw and two operators. But there is slight evidence of mechanical saws being used to cut stone in the Moselle valley, and there seems no good reason why similar machinery could not have been equally used for wood.

The removal of tree-stumps or the grubbing up of scrub required an assortment of mattocks and grub-axes as well as ordinary axes and possibly saws. Moreover, since

44

most of the ploughs then in use could only turn the soil with difficulty in order to bury the sod, with its accompanying grass and weeds, this had to be cleared as well, a process which would have been aided by various types of bladed and pronged draw-hoes, with their size and robustness matched to suit the soil type. In the same way, these implements could have been used to clear flints or lumps of rock in the topsoil, thus helping also to break up the ground before ploughing took place. Collected in baskets, these pieces of rock were usually dumped on the edges of fields, and in time helped to augment the boundaries which may have consisted of fences, or eventually hedges. On level, low-lying ground, boundaries were frequently supplemented with ditches, which also improved drainage. The spade, a Roman introduction, undoubtedly helped in their digging, and three main types have been recognized: a long-handled implement with a shield-shaped, iron blade, not unlike the modern Cornish shovel, and suitable mainly for light and loose soils; a rectangular-bladed implement made entirely of wood, which was ideal for digging heavy clay, since the blade does not become clogged with the clay; and a similarly shaped blade, shod and bound in iron, presumably to give greater strength.

Once clearance had taken place and boundaries been made, normal cultivation could start. At its most primitive this could be carried out with hoes, but ploughs were already in use in Bronze and Iron Age Britain, although it is doubtful if they were strong enough to cope with heavy soils (fig. 17). The commonest type was the bow-ard, fitted with a wooden, iron, or sometimes, as in the north of Scotland, a stone, share; iron shares varied considerably in type and size in the Roman period, ranging from a simple iron bar to a flat, flanged share which fitted round the end of the sole. Ploughs of this type were only really of use on light soils, since they did little more than shuffle the surface, which would not happen on soils with a high clay content. But when fitted with ground wrests on either side of the share, they were capable of ridging and could be used for burying seed, and if tilted while in use could turn a rudimentary furrow.

But the real improvement came with the introduction of the plough with winged share, coulter and mould-board. It used to be thought that this type was introduced during the later Iron Age, which now seems very doubtful, and it is better seen as a Roman product. Basically, the share cut a horizontal slice below the surface, and the coulter a vertical one beside it; the wooden mould-board, which was attached behind the share, then inverted the sod towards the furrow side, so burying surface grass and weeds; its cutting action meant that it could also be used on much heavier soils.

It is probable that most ploughs were drawn by oxen attached by a yoke to the plough beam, although there is no reason why other draught animals should not have been used. It also seems to have been the custom for most fields to be ploughed at least twice, sometimes in two different directions, to achieve a thorough breaking up of the soil.

The so-called 'Celtic' fields of the Iron Age in Britain were normally squarish in shape and averaged c. 0.2 ha in area, and it is usually assumed that they represented the ploughing ability of one man with one plough doing a day's work (fig. 52). They seem almost invariably to have been cross-ploughed, suggesting the use of the ard. They were generally laid out in regular blocks with boundaries of banks, ditches, fences (and hedges), heaps of stone or drystone walls. If they lay on a slope, then repeated ploughing caused soil creep, so producing the characteristic lynchets which

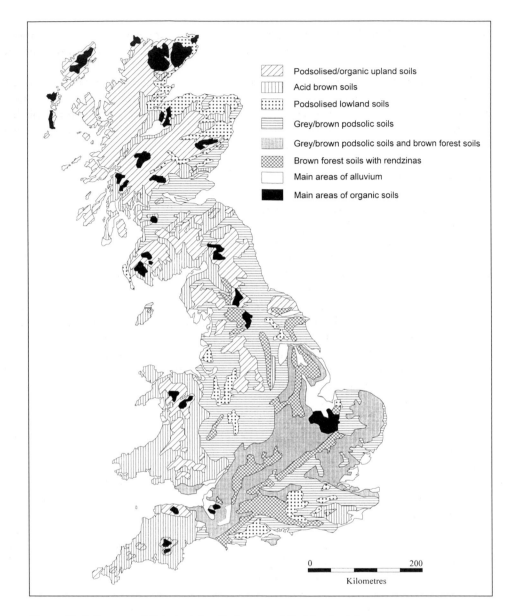

Figure 17 Soil types of Britain (after B. Jones and D. Mattingly).

mark their boundaries today. Many of these fields continued in use without alteration through the Roman period. At some sites they were replaced by larger, rectangular 'long' fields with proportions of 4 or 5:1 and up to *c.* 0.6ha in extent, and it has been argued that they represent the introduction of the plough with coulter and mould-board. A longer field would be more suitable for a heavier implement, since fewer turns would be required at the headlands. Moreover, the need for cross-ploughing would disappear. But this is probably too simplistic an explanation and the complexities incurred by trying to relate ploughs to fields were long ago summarized by Bowen (p. 127).

The creation of ridged furrows would likewise require some kind of harrow to break down the soil before sowing. The simplest form was made of stout brushwood, clasped together in a flat wooden frame which was dragged over the surface. It would probably have been ineffective on anything but the lightest and most friable soils; for heavier soils various toothed wooden harrows are thought to have existed, but there is little direct evidence. Alternatively a tilth could have been created by using hoes and rakes to break up clods.

The principal crops grown in these fields in the Iron Age have already been mentioned in Chapter 2, together with the weeds that are likely to have been seen with them. During the Roman period there was probably an increase in the cultivation of spelt, which was hardy enough to be sown in the autumn, thus increasing yields. It is also probable that more vegetables were grown, especially roots, which would provide food for both people and animals during the winter; but, of course, proportions cannot be calculated.

Larger areas were also laid down to pasture, but resemblance to modern fields with their uniform green, largely weed-free lays would have been minimal. Almost any open land, when cleared of dense scrub, was suitable, although it should be borne in mind that horses and sheep prefer short grass, while cattle will eat longer varieties; goats will browse as well as graze and pigs can be run almost anywhere, but they tend in time to destroy a pasture with their rooting. So a judicious mixture of animals would make the best use of any rough pasture.

There is a further factor involved here: the existence of poisonous plants in the herbage. Today, by far the most deadly to horses and stock is Common Ragwort, which causes half of all cases of poisoning in these animals. It is a common weed largely of hedgerow, scrub and unkempt pasture, although it will also grow in a variety of other environments, and its heads of golden-yellow flowers, standing to a metre or more, make a fine addition to the colour of the mid-summer countryside. While growing it seems to be unpalatable to stock, but when cut and dried – as in hay-making – it will be eaten readily to cause irreversible cirrhosis of the liver and ultimate death. How common it was in the prehistoric and Roman periods is difficult to assess, since it does not show readily in pollen sequences or lists of plant material. For instance it does not appear at Silchester or York, but is listed from the Upper Walbrook in London, mainly in the early and later Roman periods. Its absence from hay found at York might suggest that its poisonous properties were recognized and that it had been carefully removed either before or after harvesting; but caution should be observed since this apparent absence might simply be due to fickleness in survival or sampling. Nevertheless, the samples from London show that it was present in Roman Britain, although not perhaps as common as today; yet it seeds readily and could have posed real problems for horse and cattle owners, whether or not its poisonous properties were recognized. Other poisonous plants, which seem to have been fairly common in the same period, such as Hemlock and Deadly Nightshade, were more of a threat to children than to animals.

While rough pasture and light scrub may have been suitable for grazing, hay-meadows needed more careful management, with the removal of thick-stemmed, pulpy plants. The latter would have delayed the drying of the grass, which, if inadequate, might have caused mould growth and rotting in the final product. Nettles, however, when cut and wilted will be eaten by most animals and form a nutritious feed. Hay-meadows were also available for additional pasture, once the crop had been taken, and could be so used until the following spring.

Cereal crops, once sown, would gradually turn much of the cultivated countryside from brown to green and then to yellow, and when ripe would have added to the textural appearance, as when a wind ripples across a field of mature barley or bearded wheat. But unless weeded by hand (p. 27) such fields in ancient times were no doubt choked with other plants, which supplemented the colour and texture. Harvesting could be carried out with a variety of implements, but there is some dispute over how this was done, although it is generally agreed that the ears were cut separately and the straw mown later. 'Reaping' hooks and (more so in the Roman period) the balanced sickle were in common use from prehistoric times onwards, but doubts have been cast on their suitability for cereals, and hand-picking of the ears has been suggested as a faster alternative. Long-handled scythes are also known, some with blades up to 1.6 m long, and were no doubt used for cutting both straw and hay. Considerable skill is needed to operate blades of this length, but once perfected, harvesting could have been carried out that much more quickly. Implements of this nature are still in use in the Lower Danube valley in Romania. Some so-called 'mechanical' reapers are also attested on sculpture in Gaul, but seem to be restricted to the western empire. A draft animal pushed a small hopper, equipped on its lower edge with closely spaced projecting teeth, through the standing crop, plucking the ears of grain as it went. Such a device would have been ideal for picking up cereals which had become lodged by wind or rain, a common condition in northern Gaul and Britain; harvesting by hand, sickle or scythe under these circumstances would be difficult and wasteful. Once the crop had been carried, animals and poultry were no doubt released into the stubble to fatten on the surviving weeds and spilt grain. At the same time they manured the soil, before ploughing started once again, so bringing to an end the cycle of the changing seasons, each one of which added its own distinctive form, texture and colour to the country- side.

5

FARMS AND RELIGION
IN THE LANDSCAPE
The rural scene

The contrast between rural and urban topography only became a reality in Britain during the Roman period, with the construction of nucleated towns and villages. Undoubtedly, the emergence of towns affected the landscape, but in very restricted areas. Similarly the growth of villas and rural sanctuaries, often to replace their Iron Age equivalents, must have made some difference. Yet many areas in the north and west of Britain were devoid of villas, while the relatively small areas occupied by their buildings in the south and east would have produced little more than a series of pinpricks on the countryside. But they may have been responsible for introducing more orderliness, as the result of better management, as well as considerably more clearance for cultivation. Neither must we forget that even in the regions where villas predominated, many Iron Age farms continued largely unaltered by the growth of the new system. It can be argued, therefore, that even the growth of up to about 1,000 villas in Britain produced only a small impact on the visual appearance of the countryside.

The earliest villas were usually of simple plan, consisting of no more than a range of single-storey rooms, perhaps united by a verandah extending the length of the building. Local materials were invariably used in the construction, which may have been of half-timber based on a low masonry sleeper wall (fig. 18). Thus in the south-east and most of East Anglia the masonry was mainly composed of flint, with occasionally brick being used for quoins and jambs. This gave way to the oolites of the Jurassic zone, running north-east from Somerset up to and slightly beyond the Humber, although Lincolnshire and east Yorkshire could also provide flint from the chalk Wolds. In the remaining parts, where villas tended to be few, a variety of sandstones, gritstones and metamorphic or igneous rocks were employed. The skills needed to dress the latter had not been developed; consequently they were used in nodular form, not unlike flint. The most noticeable feature of these buildings might have been roofs of red tile, had these been used, although thatch was no doubt an alternative in the simpler forms, with diamond-shaped slates of oolite or sandstone available in appropriate areas.

The majority of villas were sited near valley bottoms, or on the lower slopes of hills. There are exceptions such as that at Scampton, north of Lincoln, which lay just below the top of the western edge of the limestone scarp. The overriding conditions seem to have been proximity to a good water supply and shelter; the latter depended on the part of the country in which the villa was situated. Thus the villas lying, as at Scampton, along the western edge of the Lincolnshire limestone were to some degree protected from the bitterly cold north-east and east winter winds, for which

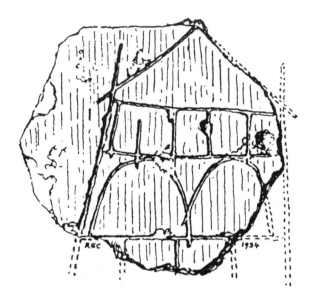

Figure 18 A representation of the gable end of a half-timbered house scratched on wall plaster from the villa at Hucclecote near Gloucester (first drawn by R.G. Collingwood and published in the *Journal of Roman Studies*, 24 (1934)).

Lincolnshire is noted. In contrast, the position of the villa at Chedworth, in the heart of the Cotswolds, in an eastern-facing comb, ensured that it did not receive the full force of the prevailing westerlies in that part of the country. Consequently most villas will have only been seen from their surrounding hills, unless situated as on the Lincolnshire limestone or the Fen edge, when they would have been visible for far greater distances and thus exerted a greater impact on the landscape.

The houses themselves provided form, texture and colour. Based on rectangles or squares, a shape unknown in nature, they would have cut across the natural contours of the ground and vegetation, thus creating an immediately visible contrast. Texture, when seen from a distance, would have come primarily from the type of roofing material – tiles, thatch or slates. From nearer by, the walls would exert a greater influence – rough masonry of different kinds of stone, exposed half-timbering, smooth lime-washed plaster covering all or part of the wall. The same factors would have governed colour: patches of red (or very rarely yellow) from tiles, golden-yellow from fresh thatch, fading quickly to greyish-brown, and a variety of reddish-browns, greys, greens or yellows from slates, also changing colour slowly as weathering took place. Associated farm buildings added their own elements to the scene, while the nearest fields and enclosures would have provided a patchwork of seasonal changes, surrounded by hedges, fences or drystone walls (fig. 19).

By the second century villas were becoming larger and more elaborate; a few possessed mosaics and bath wings, while the basic architectural form was changing. In many cases they now had wings projecting from the ends of the main ranges of rooms. Where suitable stone was available, verandah posts of wood were replaced by small columns; thatched roofs probably gave way to more permanent tiles or slates. Some

Figure 19 Reconstruction drawing of a villa at Whitton (S. Wales) (after Jarrett).

were enclosed within their own farmyards, containing barns, byres and other installations. This expansion was presumably brought about by increasing wealth, which in
turn probably reflected greater areas under cultivation and pasture, with larger yields
and bigger herds and flocks.

Typical of this period of development is a group of villas not far from Verulamium
at Park Street, Gorhambury and Lockleys, all of which replaced typical late Iron Age
farmhouses with simple buildings of romanized form. At Ditchley (Oxon.), a
rectangular timber-framed house of first-century date was rebuilt in masonry, or half-
timbering, to the winged corridor pattern, in the early second century. But it is useless
to be dogmatic about the typology of development, since each villa represented the
personal circumstances and inclinations of the tenant or owner; there could, therefore,
be theoretically as many variations in villa type as there were villas in Britain, and, in
a way, it is surprising that there is any conformity at all. That there was so much was
partly due to the availability of standard plans, to fashion and a desire to keep up with,
or surpass, the Julii next door. Moreover, estates could be bought and sold, leased out
to tenants, run by a resident manager, combined or split up, all circumstances which
would affect the domestic residence at the centre, which could be occupied, or left
unoccupied to fall into ruin, as happened in some cases. But each and every one of
these cases would have had some sort of impact on the surrounding countryside; a
derelict building, perhaps minus its roof and surrounded by a new growth of weeds
and scrub, would look very different from the trim appearance of an occupied residence.

51

By the fourth century many villas had grown even larger, pointing towards a considerable consolidation of land-holdings into very large estates. It is very difficult to say how these were managed. Some may have been let out to tenants, such as might be the case where one or two smaller villas exist at no great distance from a larger one. Others may have been run by bailiffs with a large workforce of slaves or serfs, as at Hambledon (Bucks.); by now there was little difference between these classes, since most of the peasantry was bound to the land by debt.

In many instances the original winged-corridor type of villa had expanded so that a central courtyard became entirely enclosed by buildings, as at North Leigh (Oxon.), or at least on three sides, with the fourth shut off by a wall, as at Spoonley Wood (Glos.). In some of the very largest villas, another courtyard was constructed beyond the first, as at Bignor (Sussex), while at Woodchester (Glos.) there are strong suggestions of even a third. The functions of these courtyards have long been disputed. Where only one existed, it is probable that it was primarily the farmyard, although parts may have been laid out as a garden. Where there was more than one, it would seem that the activities of the farm had been displaced into the outer courtyard and that the inner was retained solely as a garden, where flowers and possibly fruit and vegetables could be cultivated. These arrangements can to some degree be matched by the associated buildings. With a single courtyard, those furthest from the residence appear more like barns or byres, which were usually banished to the outer courtyard when one existed.

The existence of gardens is difficult to prove on excavation, although flower-beds have been postulated for some areas immediately outside the farmhouse at Frocester (Glos.), while cultivated strips have been identified in Colchester. The prime example, however, is the great house at Fishbourne (Sussex), which may have been the palace of the client king Cogidubnus, and which was built in the later decades of the first century. Here the central area was bisected by a walk flanked by pergolas and parterres, with recessed alcoves, which also extended around the perimeter of the courtyard. The remaining areas seem to have been maintained either as the then fashionable 'wild' garden or as lawns; parts may have been under more regulated cultivation, since a water supply had been inserted, probably also providing water for fountains or other aquatic features. Smaller, more private gardens were situated within the north and east wings, with another, much larger, stretching southwards from the south wing towards the water.

It is not difficult to visualize the appearance of a garden like that at Fishbourne, since there are a number of surviving wall-paintings, notably the Garden Room of the House of Livia in Rome; this depicts just such a scene as might have been represented by the broad walk at Fishbourne, with its elements of formality allied to 'wild' areas. Pliny gives a detailed description of his own gardens in Italy, with the emphasis on contrasts between light and shade, formal and natural. What is more difficult is to identify the typical plants which might have grown at, for instance, Fishbourne. Pollen analysis of the soils from the bedding trenches was not helpful, revealing only the hardier weeds of cultivation, such as hawkweed and daisy. It was suggested by the excavator that the parterres were composed of box, which was certainly grown then in Britain and box clippings have been found in garden waste at Silchester; but there are objections to this view, even though box has been used in the restored garden on the site. The only other direct evidence for plant remains was a jar of seeds from a climbing, everlasting pea (*Lathyrus sp.*), which is still grown today, and would have been ideal for covering trellis or pergola with masses of pink blossoms in summer, although the whole plant dies down to the ground in winter. Other plants would almost certainly have included roses, which Pliny mentions as growing on pergolas, while many fruit trees, such as pear, apple, cherry and gages, can be trained as espaliers against a wall or trellis. Many British wild plants, such as foxgloves, mallow, St John's Wort, marjoram, thyme, strawberry and violet, not only added visual interest when introduced to a formal garden, but would also be useful for culinary or medicinal purposes, while a variety of trees such as blackthorn, hazel, elderberry, bullace and bramble would provide fruit and nuts. To this list must be added species generally acknowledged to have been Roman introductions: mulberry, damson, vine and walnut; the vegetables carrot, radish, turnip, pea and corn-salad; the pot-herbs alexanders, fennel, chervil, coriander and dill, the opium poppy with its showy white, pink or red flowers would make a dramatic splash of colour in a garden, followed first by the unripened seed capsules, which provided the drug, and then by the non-toxic ripe seeds used in cooking. Another likely introduction is the wild gladiolus, *gladiolus illyricum*, which is now naturalized over much of the west country, and also in much of the Mediterranean. Admittedly, it has been grown commercially here in more recent times, but its origins may lie in the Mediterranean trade of the Roman, or even pre-Roman period. It must also be remembered that the rigid separation between flower and vegetable gardens often observed today probably did not apply in Roman times. Many vegetables can in themselves provide structure and variations in texture and colour when grown among purely ornamental flowers and shrubs. The only disadvantage in this method would seem to be when it comes to harvesting, which must have been more time-consuming. Such a garden, enclosed on all sides by buildings, can have had little impact on the visual appearance of the countryside, but in itself would have provided a great deal. In high summer the predominant colour would have been green, in all the varieties of textures presented by different types of foliage. Green, at the centre of the spectrum, is the most restful of colours, and when enlivened by splashes of muted or more vibrant shades from flowers, and combined with aquatic features, must have provided a delightful haven, in which the owner and his family could relax from the cares and tribulations of official duties. In the other seasons of the year, the appropriate colour and textural changes would give a variable interest which is the principal joy of any garden.

But villas and native-style farms were not the only buildings to be found in the countryside of Roman Britain. There were also many rural temples and bigger religious sites, as well as, notably in the south-east, large burial mounds, often arranged in groups. One of the best examples of the latter is the group of eight barrows that was arranged in two lines on the Bartlow Hills in Essex; unfortunately only four now survive. The largest rose to a height of nearly 14m, with a basal diameter of 44m. The group appears to have been related to a very large nearby villa and probably represents family burials of some richness. As objects in the landscape, they must have formed dominating features, especially when first erected, with the whiteness of the chalk mounds visible from some distance, until, as grass grew, they merged more with their background. Another group of six barrows lines the main road at Stevenage (Herts.) and must have been a useful landmark for the traveller.

Other barrows and mausolea in the countryside were usually situated adjacent to villas, and presumably represented the burials of residents. One remarkable example was built in the early fourth century behind the villa at Lullingstone (Kent). It was planned like a Romano-Celtic temple with the 'cella' containing the tomb chamber, in which were two coffins and an array of grave goods; it seems to have had a domed or vaulted roof, coated externally with pink *opus signinum*, and must have risen to a height of 5 m or more above ground level. Since it also occupied a higher terrace to the west of the main house, it was the most prominent object in the group of buildings visible for some distance in most directions.

There were many rural temples and shrines in Roman Britain, some creating sizeable settlements around them, such as Bath, Frilford, Springhead and Wycomb; but these more rightly belong in the category of towns. Other solitary examples are truly rural, and undoubtedly the greatest effect on the landscape was made by those situated on the hilltops, often inside disused hillforts, such as Maiden Castle, Chanctonbury (fig. 3) and Lydney. Many of them were late foundations and probably represent a return to older, religious values at a time when Christianity was in the ascendant.

The forms which these temples took were varied, although the commonest, certainly in the south, was the Romano-Celtic; this consisted of a central, usually square but sometimes circular, tower-like 'cella' surrounded by a verandah. The form was also common to parts of Gaul and Germany and some were of considerable size, rising to heights of 25 m, but it is unlikely that such magnitude was to be observed in Britain. The temple at Maiden Castle had a 'cella' less than 5 m sq. and is unlikely to have risen much more in height. Neither was it situated on the highest part of the hillfort and it is possible that the roof was not even visible above the surrounding Iron Age ramparts. At first it appears to have been roofed with hexagonal limestone slates, which would have provided a subdued colour but a characteristic texture to its appearance; later these were replaced by tiles, thus changing both colour and texture to a marked degree. The exterior of the verandah wall was plastered and painted yellow above a dado splashed with red, but no evidence was found that the cella walls were similarly treated, although its interior was decorated with multi-coloured panels of bluish-green, dark red and white.

But most temples and shrines lay in valleys, such as that at Uley, near Cirencester, and Thistleton (Rutland). Sometimes, though, they were accompanied by other buildings, such as a house for a resident priest, or, in the case of very popular shrines, by a theatre or amphitheatre, as at Frilford, or Gosbecks, near Colchester. Exceptional in this context were those situated in the depths of the countryside, like that which must have existed at Bollihope Common, near Stanhope (Durham), where was found the altar erected to commemorate the killing of a wild boar 'of exceptional fineness'. The area must then have been wooded. Similar shrines, one circular, the other rectangular, have been found at Scargill Moor, near Bowes (Durham); whether or how they were roofed is not known. Altars found in them were dedications to Vinotonus.

These rural shrines and temples, because of their very solitariness, will have had a major effect on the landscape, enhanced if they were situated on a hilltop, but more muted if they were buried in a woodland grove. If they were roofed, texture would have been provided by tiles or slates, and, if left unrendered, by the nature of the walls. Similarly colour will have come in the same way, with tiles giving a splash of red in otherwise mainly green surroundings. Rendered walls were probably given a lime-wash, perhaps coloured, thus enhancing their visibility from a distance, with the general whiteness, but fading to grey or green with age.

One last example is worth mentioning. At the east end of the Antonine Wall, near Falkirk and beyond the Wall, a domed shrine now known as Arthur's O'on was built. Unfortunately it was dismantled in the eighteenth century and the stone used to build a mill-dam. But once it must have dominated the surrounding landscape and been visible for many kilometres. It appears to have been associated with Winged Victories and legionary eagles, and probably commemorated the successful completion of the Scottish War, conducted by Lollius Urbicus, which culminated in the construction of the new frontier.

6

URBAN TOPOGRAPHY
AND HUMAN SENSATIONS

Together with the military installations, the growth of urban centres was a completely new experience for Britain during the Roman period. It has been claimed that there were towns in Iron Age Britain, but these were very different in appearance. They much resembled other Iron Age settlements outwardly but with a greater density of buildings. The materials of construction and the form of the houses remained very similar. Consequently the arrival in Britain of closely spaced rectangular buildings was a considerable departure from what had gone before, and had a greater effect on the landscape, since straight lines and right angles are foreign to nature, whereas curves are not; however, they were restricted to some two dozen major and seventy to eighty minor towns.

Most of the new sites were situated on low-lying ground, often on flood plains of rivers, such as Cirencester, Winchester, Canterbury and Chichester. Some, like London, Dorchester, Exeter, Colchester and York, were placed on raised geological features close to rivers, and others, as with Verulamium, on valley slopes. Most of the major towns, and many of the minor, owed much to early military sites and the vici that grew beside them, such as Cirencester, Dorchester-on-Thames, Great Casterton and Ancaster, or to existing native settlements, as with Braughing; a few had origins in both, as at Canterbury, Leicester and Silchester. Exceptionally, some, as with the three new coloniae, took over the sites of abandoned legionary fortresses; this also occurred at the non-colonial sites of Exeter and Wroxeter. Only very occasionally were they placed on a hilltop, like Lincoln (fig. 20), which inherited the fortress situated on the spur of the limestone ridge overlooking the valley of the river Witham; even here though it ultimately spilled down the hillside to the water's edge (fig. 21). Most sites were, therefore, ideally placed for the supply of water, and for drainage of both surface water and excess from an aqueduct; the nearby river often also provided a convenient transport link, which in some cases gave rise, as at Gloucester, Lincoln and London, to considerable lengths of quays and the growth of a flourishing water-borne trade.

At the peak of the urban hierarchy were the chartered towns, the *coloniae* and *municipia*. The former, as far as we know, numbered Colchester, Lincoln, Gloucester, and later York, although London too may have become a colonia in the fourth century, after having been first promoted to a municipium; other promotions are a possibility. The municipia almost certainly included Verulamium, although there is no direct evidence, and it has been suggested that some other towns, such as Canterbury and Dorchester, were subsequently raised to this rank, since they lacked the tribal suffix in

Figure 20 An impression of the upper town at Lincoln, with the aqueduct running towards the town from the north-east (reproduced by the kind permission of David Vale and FLARE).

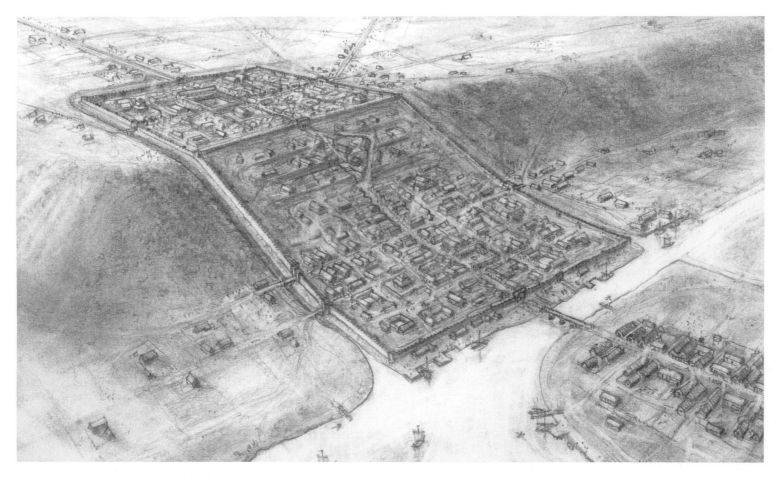

Figure 21 An impression of the lower town at Lincoln, which ultimately spilt down the hillside to the water's edge of the river Witham (reproduced by the kind permission of David Vale and FLARE).

some documentary sources, which was normally accorded to civitas capitals. All these chartered towns represented the highest degree of *romanitas* in Britain and probably contained the greatest proportion of classically inspired buildings.

Next we descend through the ranks of civitas capitals, which at the top of the scale were probably little different in visual appearance from the chartered towns; some certainly exceeded the latter in size, such as Cirencester, capital of the Dobunni, and Wroxeter, capital of the Cornovii (fig. 22). At the lower end of the scale, there were towns like Carmarthen, capital of the south-west Welsh civitas of the Demetae, and Caistor-by-Norwich, head of the Iceni, which probably differed little from some of the larger minor towns, such as Towcester, Water Newton and Ilchester; it has been argued that the last two sites were later promoted to act as capitals for newly constituted civitates. Nevertheless, if that had been so, there were still significant differences between them and the earlier examples.

There were two fundamental aspects of most of the towns both major and minor: with or without defences. Once defences were built, particularly walls, few of the internal buildings would have been seen from the outside, since most were only a single storey high and would be hidden from sight. Visual aspects would also change with the situation. Towns built on reasonably level ground, as the majority were, would have seemed much the same from whichever angle they were viewed. When built on sloping ground, such as Verulamium, they would have provided a panorama when seen from the opposing hill, with most of the interior visible even above the defences, albeit in a foreshortened manner. If built on a slight eminence, such as Colchester (fig. 23) or London, a near view would have revealed little more than the defences, tops of higher buildings and roofs, while hilltop towns like Lincoln, in its original form, would have shown little more than the walls and some rooftops; a panoramic view would have been almost impossible to obtain, or a sight of the inner buildings.

But before defences were built, obscuring much of the interior, all would have presented a very different sight, unique to each place, but with points of similarity. The principal form of major towns was imparted by the streets and public buildings. The streets were usually arranged in a regular plan, dividing the land into rectangular *insulae*. Normally there were two main streets, the *cardo* and the *decumanus*, intersecting near the centre; in one of the corners so formed, the forum and basilica would usually be placed with the latter facing a southerly aspect, although this was not always the case. The forum consisted of an open courtyard surrounded by two or three ranges of shops or offices, with an internal, and sometimes external, colonnade, such as occurs at Cirencester. The basilica, along the fourth side, was a large aisled hall with a range of rooms along the outside. From architectural fragments recovered in excavations, the height might be anything up to 15 m and the length, as at London (the largest in Britain), over 160 m. It was therefore the biggest and probably the most dominant building in the town, and would have appeared in much the same relation to the remaining buildings as cathedrals did in medieval towns, visible from most aspects. Lighting of the nave was provided by clerestory windows, which were spaced at intervals along the upper levels, so providing some relief in an otherwise blank wall. The roofs may have been vaulted internally, but more likely had a beamed ceiling which could be plastered and perhaps painted to imitate coffering. Externally they were probably clad in whatever material was used locally for roofing, probably tiles or

WROXETER (Viroconivm)

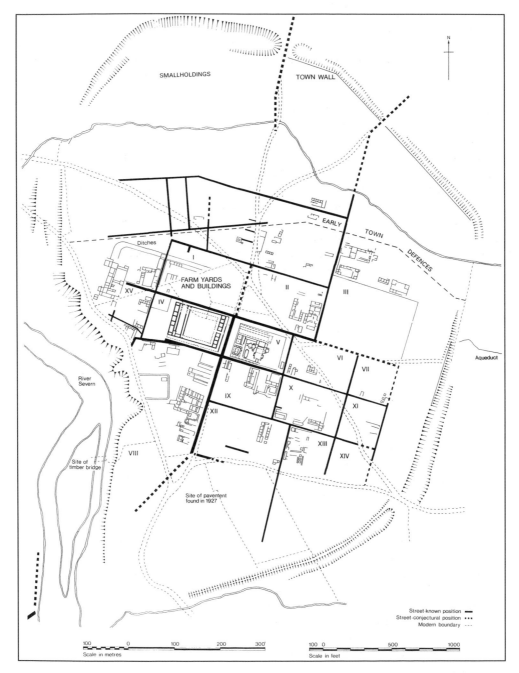

Figure 22 Plan of the Roman town of Wroxeter (after Webster and Barker).

slates; there is some suggestion from Cirencester that lead was used for the apse at the south-west end, so providing a ribbed, smooth grey appearance and contrasting in both colour and texture with the red, brown or greenish-grey of tiles or slates.

Another prominent building present in major towns and also in some minor ones was the bath-house. Its situation was more variable than that of the forum and basilica, and depended on the water supply and adequate drainage. Thus although the bath-house occupied positions next to the forum at Leicester, Exeter and Chichester, it was several insulae away at Silchester, while the Huggin Hill bath-house in London was placed against the slope of the gravel bank, on which the city lies, near the south-west corner and overlooking the Thames, and from which it drew its water.

Bath-houses were massive buildings with thick walls, not only to support the heavy superstructure, but also to insulate against heat loss. Their nature meant that they were always built in stone and brick or a combination of both, and they were often the earliest masonry buildings in a town. They were subject to frequent reconstructions of the hot rooms, which was caused by expansion and contraction of the walls due to rapid changes in temperature and unequal distribution of heat. The walls of an experimental bath-house built at Xanten in Germany had cracked above the furnace end after only a few years' use (fig. 24).

Local stone was normally employed in the construction, but arches and corners were often turned in brick, especially in the south-east where flint was the usual building medium; brick string courses were also found. The same procedure was followed in the bath-house at Leicester, where the local stone was not easily worked; a large fragment of wall still stands to some height and is composed predominately of green and grey Charnwood granites and slates, allied with some sandstone and limestone, but with architectural pieces of millstone grit from Derbyshire. A considerable amount of brick was used for arches and corners. Similar methods were employed in the standing wall at Wroxeter, although here the principal building stone was red sandstone. Walls were occasionally covered internally with veneers of imported, exotic stones such as porphyry and marbles. Roofs of larger bath-houses were normally vaulted to withstand the temperature and humidity. Sometimes they contained ducts to carry the furnace gases, which travelled up from the hypocausts through wall channels; vents in the vaulting presumably then had to be provided. Sometimes also these vaults were constructed with tufa voussoirs, which not only lightened the weight, but also, because of their vesicular nature, provided better insulation. But in lighter constructions, such as that at Silchester, where the walls do not seem strong enough to stand the weight of vaults, the hot rooms may have been roofed after the Vitruvian method with ceilings formed of large flat tiles attached to rafters and heavily plastered.

Vaults of bath-houses may have been left exposed to view, or more possibly they were covered by a timber frame to support a tile roof, as in the reconstruction drawing of that at Leicester (fig. 25). They would certainly have risen to some height, although perhaps not as high as the basilica; much would depend on the scale of the building. Moreover, some bath-houses in Britain possessed covered exercise halls in place of normally open-air *palaestrae* as at Leicester and Wroxeter. These may have risen higher than the remainder of the building and perhaps vied with the basilica for dominance. The external appearance of the whole building will, of course, have been conditioned by the treatment of the outside walls. Some modern reconstructions show them rendered and lime-washed, but this seems unlikely for the originals. The care with

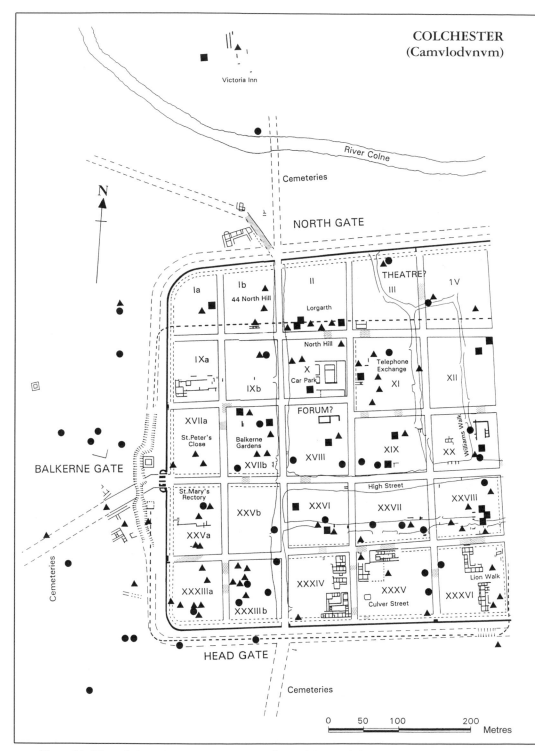

Figure 23 Plan of the colonia at Colchester (after Niblett and Crummy).

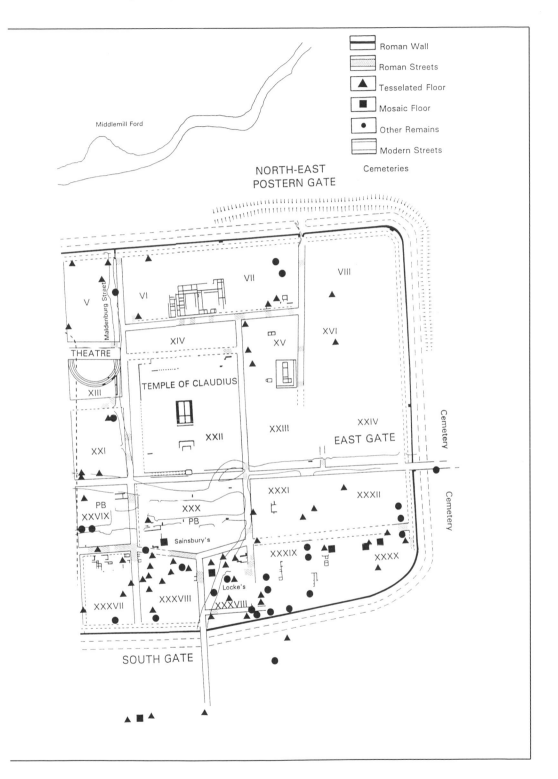

Figure 24 Cracked wall in the furnace room of the reconstructed bath-house at Xanten in Germany.

which facing stones were cut and laid suggests that they were meant to be seen, although this may not have been so where flint or other rough material was used. The latter seems to have been true of Silchester, where it was recorded that the external faces of the walls were plastered, but there is no mention of a lime-wash. It was also found that here the entrance portico was made of Bath stone, so that classical features were incorporated that would have clashed badly with unrendered walls of flint and rough stone.

Other buildings that may have provided height to the visual aspect of towns were theatres and amphitheatres. While the latter are known from almost every major town, the former were confined to a small number: so far only Canterbury, Verulamium, Colchester and Brough-on-Humber have produced evidence for them. Although the Verulamium theatre was comparatively small in scale, being only some 58 m in diameter in its last phase, the second theatre at Canterbury was almost half as big again at 80 m. Fragments of column from the stage area at Verulamium suggest an overall height of about 8–10 m, so, although it would rise above surrounding buildings, which were, at the most, only two storeys high, it would not have the same visual impact as the nearby basilica. The Canterbury theatre (fig. 26) on the other hand must have been a good deal higher, because of its greater diameter; moreover, the thickness of its walls – the outer wall of the *cavea* was nearly 4 m thick – would imply a massive superstructure. It could, therefore, compete more closely with the basilica in height. The theatre at Colchester was estimated to be *c.* 65 m in diameter, and would not have risen quite so high, but high enough to have appeared above surrounding

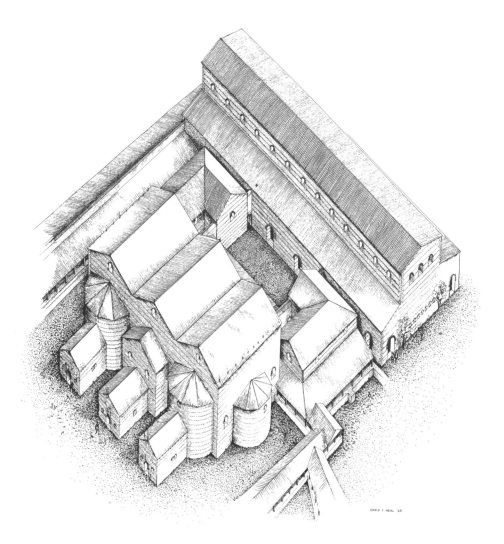

Figure 25 Reconstruction drawing of the bath-house at Leicester (drawing by David Neal).

buildings, except perhaps for the Temple of Claudius and its associated structures, and the basilica, the site of which is not yet known (fig. 27). A theatre is also suspected at Lincoln, possibly built into the slope of the hillside, against which the seats of the cavea would have been backed. Consequently, it would not have made a great impact on the landscape, with only the walls of the stage buildings rising free of the hill. Theatres and amphitheatres were often constructed in this manner in the empire, which resulted in a considerable economy in the masonry; one of the best examples is at Lyon (Lugdunum) in Gallia Lugdunensis, where both theatres were built against the hill known as Fourvière.

In appearance, most theatres were built of local stone; thus at Canterbury walls of flint and brick formed the cores, although there is some evidence to show that the

Figure 26 Reconstruction drawing of the centre of Roman Canterbury. The theatre stands in the middle, facing the temple precinct, which is part of the forum and basilica complex. To the near right are the vaulted roofs of a bath-house, drawn in contrast to the tiled finish given to the roof of the Leicester bath-house (fig. 25) (reproduced by the kind permission of the Canterbury Archaeological Trust and John Bowen).

Figure 27 Reconstruction drawing of Colchester from the south-west (reproduced by the kind permission of the Colchester Archaeological Trust and Peter Froste).

exterior was, at least, faced with Kentish rag. At Colchester, septaria was used, so that the outer appearance would have been brownish. Presumably, since they were essentially classical buildings, they would have been ornamented in an appropriate style. The architectural fragments at Verulamium suggest that the Corinthian order was used.

Amphitheatres are more widely known: London, Chichester, Cirencester, Dorchester, Carmarthen, Caerwent and possibly Leicester possessed them, while an odd structure at Wroxeter and a very small possible example at Caister-by-Norwich have been associated with amphitheatrical displays. They are sometimes found at minor towns such as at the mining settlement of Charterhouse-on-Mendip, and also at Richborough, although in both cases they may have been primarily provided for military garrisons. Normally, in Britain they were situated on the outskirts of the main built-up areas, although the late example at Caerwent was placed nearer the town centre; it was, though, much smaller than usual, and did not take up so much space, which was the reason why most were banished to the outskirts. The amphitheatre at London was also found inside the town, near the south-eastern corner of the fort; again it may have military connexions. The amphitheatre, therefore, was the major building to be seen in the suburbs of a town, but probably not rising as high as a theatre. At first, most were built with timber retaining earth seating banks, but the walls were, except at Dorchester, later mostly replaced by masonry. The visual appearance of an elliptical outside wall, an unusual shape in the Roman world, built of local stone, was relieved by the opposing arena entrances at the ends of the long axis and by entrances for the audience round the remainder; the latter presumably gave access to flights of stairs, but whether they were situated within or outside the seating bank is not always clear. Neither do we know whether, or to what degree, the stonework was left exposed. There is evidence from Cirencester that the arena walls in some phases were not only plastered but also painted a variety of colours with multi-colour splashings to imitate marble. But they would not have been visible from outside, and there is no evidence to show if the exterior walls were similarly treated.

Other major buildings in urban contexts in Britain were mostly temples, either of classical or Romano-Celtic form. Classical temples, with their columned porticoes, although less common, must have exerted a greater effect on the visual appearance, since they were often constructed of stone which was not native to a locality, and raised above surrounding buildings on a podium. In some towns they were probably the most prominent feature; thus little could compete in height with the tetrastyle temple of Sulis Minerva at Bath, while the great octastyle Temple of Claudius at Colchester must have risen at least as high as the basilica (fig. 27).

Reference has already been made to the grid of streets that in major towns subdivided the land into insulae. But the street grid did not always reach a town's boundaries, as at Cirencester, while in contrast at Wroxeter it was later extended in the northern part of the town by a grid on a different alignment to the original. Nor was it always regular in layout, as at Canterbury (fig. 28), where considerable varieties occur in the size and shape of insulae, to take into account pre-existing buildings. Also, when defences were constructed, parts of a grid might be left outside them, as at Silchester, where streets on the north-west side were omitted, and at Canterbury where the suburb beyond the river Stour was likewise excluded. These variations must reflect the history of development. In some cases the original grid was obviously laid out only to encompass the central built-up area, which never expanded by much; in others,

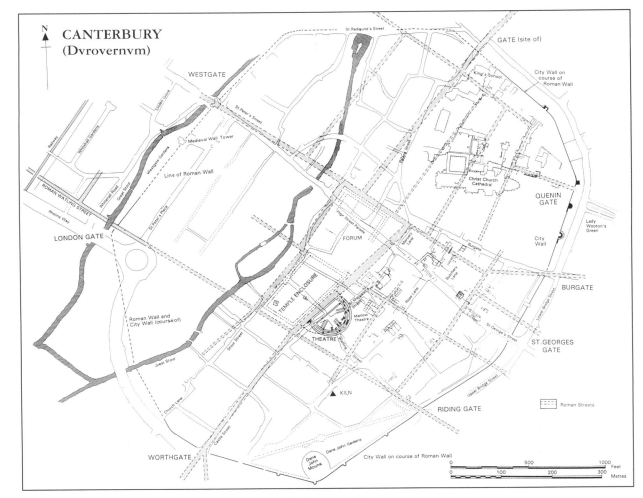

Figure 28 Plan of the Roman town of Canterbury (after Frere and Bennett).

LINCOLN (Lindum)

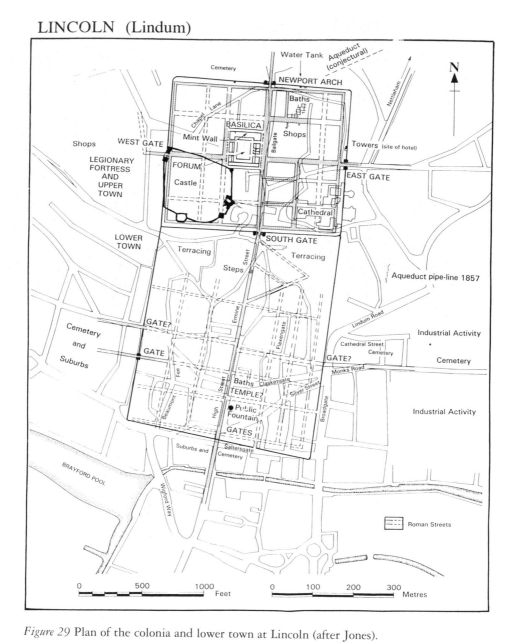

Figure 29 Plan of the colonia and lower town at Lincoln (after Jones).

expansion became necessary; while in the third case, parts were either never used, or had become uninhabited by the time fortifications were built. Nevertheless, extensive suburbs existed in many towns, either being developed after the defences had been constructed, or consisting of houses and shops which were deemed not worthy of being protected. However, in contrast at Lincoln (fig. 29), the original southern suburb on the hillside became sufficiently large and important to warrant its own defensive

Figure 30 Fallen wall in Building VI.5 at Cirencester; the gaps between the blocks of masonry mark the original positions of the timber uprights (reproduced by the kind permission of the Corinium Museum and Alan McWhirr).

system; but it was an exception in Britain. The density of building tended mainly to decline towards the outskirts, even when suburbs existed, and only the town centres were intensively developed.

The vernacular buildings consisted chiefly of houses, shops and workshops, which rarely extended above the ground floor and a single upper storey. At first, even in the coloniae, they were constructed with timber frames and wattle-and-daub panels; some, such as those at Colchester and Gloucester, had low masonry sleeper walls to support the frames; in this they were following the military tradition of their fortress predecessors. It is doubtful if these walls were ever visible, since the whole exterior was plastered and probably lime-washed. Occasionally, unbaked clay bricks were used in place of wattle-and-daub, although the final treatment, and therefore appearance, would have been similar. The majority of timber-framed buildings were founded on sleeper beams set in the ground.

Later buildings were more likely to be constructed of masonry, although these may have incorporated a degree of half-timbering. A fallen wall from a third-century half-timbered building in Cirencester (fig. 30) showed how some were constructed, with wooden uprights, spaced at *c.* 0.75 m apart, set in the thickness of the wall. The intervening spaces had been filled with coursed tile and stone. While the stone was almost always local, there is some evidence that even these buildings, as in the one quoted above at Cirencester, were rendered on the outside and sometimes painted to relieve the ubiquitous white wash. Another building, also at Cirencester, was so treated, although admittedly the wall was protected from the worst of the weather by a portico. Nevertheless, faint traces of a painted pattern could be made out.

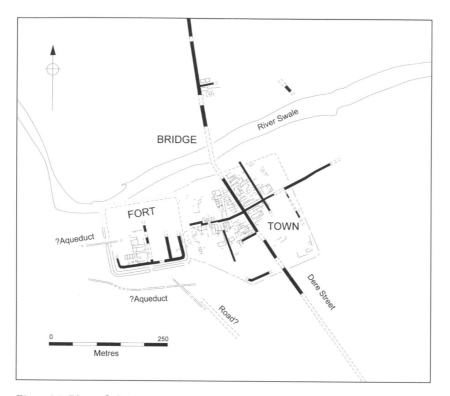

Figure 31 Plan of the Roman town at Catterick (reproduced by the kind permission of Pete Wilson and the Central Excavation Services of English Heritage).

Roofs of all types of building, whether timber-framed, half-timbered or masonry, were normally of tiles or slates, depending on the part of the country; this did not prevent, however, tiles from being used in good stone country, and some of the largest tile factories were situated on the fringe of the Cotswolds near Cirencester. But thatch may have been a cheaper alternative in poorer-quality houses.

Thus in most towns, both early and late, the predominant colour and texture was governed by a number of factors: lime-wash of varying shades of whiteness, depending on its freshness; exposed stone, changing from flint and brick in the south-east, to pale yellow in the Cotswolds and Lincolnshire, to brown in ironstone country, and red or dark red in sandstone regions; all topped off by red tiles, or slates of different hues, darkening with exposure to the weather and the growth of moss, lichens and algae. As today, and as already remarked, it was probably likely that travellers would be able to tell through which part of the country they were passing by observing the appearance of the buildings around them.

The treatment of vernacular buildings takes us logically to the minor towns, since they contained very similar building types, and the factors governing their external appearance would have been repeated. The principal difference in these minor towns was the less-orderly arrangement of streets and the lack of a regular grid, although some such as Catterick (fig. 31), Corbridge, Alchester and Ilchester possess the rudiments of one. More normal, however, were those like Kenchester, Water Newton (fig. 32) and

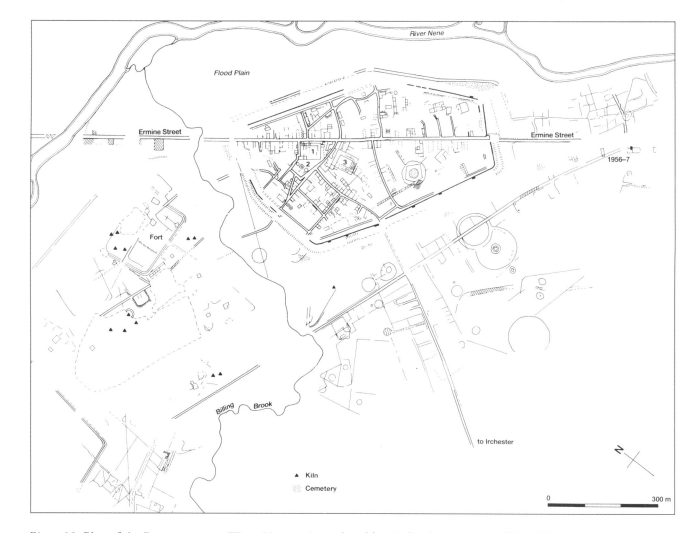

Figure 32 Plan of the Roman town at Water Newton (reproduced by the kind permission of Barry Burnham).

Wanborough among fortified sites, and Camerton, Hibaldstow and Sapperton, which were not defended, where the town had grown up along a main road. In these cases shops and houses would be concentrated along the frontages, with subsidiary roads and lanes leading off to the rear of the premises and to other buildings placed further away; these lanes would be constructed as and where the need arose. A further distinction in minor towns can be observed in the lack of public buildings, such as a basilica, although even here one cannot be dogmatic. Godmanchester possessed a basilica-like building in the third century, but it is more probable to have been associated with adjacent imperial estates. *Mansiones*, often accompanied by bath-houses, are known in a number of sites such as Catterick, Wanborough and Godmanchester; the bath-houses would have lent height to an otherwise comparatively uniform level. Otherwise height was obtained from temples, theatres and amphitheatres, and a number of minor towns grew up as religious centres. Foremost among them, as already indicated, was Bath with its great classical temple and associated hot baths, but Wycomb and Frilford both possessed theatres or amphitheatres as well as Romano-Celtic temples set in precincts. The industrial site of Charterhouse-in-Mendip contained an amphitheatre. But it is more likely to have been related to an army detachment running the silver/lead mines. In other respects, most minor towns resembled their regional major counterparts in both colour and texture.

One of the problems connected with all towns relates to the degree of vegetational cover. Tree-root cavities have been found at Carlisle and Leicester, where at the latter site a tree was cut down to build the basilica. But such evidence is scarce and is difficult to distinguish from animal burrows; it shows best when the stump was sealed by a hard impenetrable material like rammed gravel or concrete, so that a hollow is formed as the wood rotted. But we must envisage other trees in likely places; orchards may have occupied open areas in insulae, while self-sown seedlings of trees such as alder, blackthorn and hawthorn spring up surprisingly quickly on waste ground and in odd corners, and can become quite large unless kept in check by vigorous pruning or felling.

One thing is certain, however. There would have been a massive growth of annual and perennial weeds and grass along street edges, building lines, drainage ditches and waste ground. We know of several of the commonest weeds, such as plantain, butter-cup and chickweed, in pollen and waterlogged remains from Silchester, London and York (see Appendix), while an interesting experiment was carried out at Cirencester (already referred to on p. 39). Some soil deep in the Flavian levels of the excavations, and thus carefully uncontaminated by modern seeds, was submitted to germination tests. First it was chilled for some months, then allowed to germinate naturally. A fine crop of nettles was the result, showing that at least these weeds were current in that period and that the seeds had lain dormant for the best part of 1,900 years; nettles grow on waste ground and old building sites, on areas rich in phosphates from animal and human occupation, so we can assume that for a time this site lay vacant. How this weed growth was dealt with in the absence of modern weed-killers is not known, but some control would have been necessary if a town was not to become almost completely submerged during the summer months. Presumably cutting or weeding by hand was carried out where it was needed, although it is surprising how weeds, particularly flat-leaved varieties, can take root on even well-used surfaces such as streets and paths; there was no asphalt or tar-macadam to prevent growth, and even this is not always effective, since some plants can either grow in it or push their way through it. Surprisingly this aspect seldom features in reconstruction drawings, where sites are often displayed weed-free and tidy, probably the reverse of the real situation. Towns were probably much greener than we realise. Moreover, there was always the problem of mud, which must have aided weed growth. This was formed by the passage of carts, animals and people along the streets, so wearing the surfaces to dust in dry weather and mud when it rained. At times this material accumulated several centimetres thick, especially at the edges, before a new surface was laid down, a fairly frequent recurrence. The constant rise in street levels caused by this process must have been a considerable inconvenience for householders and shopkeepers, for eventually the levels must have risen higher than their thresholds, causing the mud or dust and water to enter their premises unless remedial steps were taken. Indeed the streets of towns probably left much to be desired, for not only was there the dust or mud, but also dung from passing animals, rotting vegetation and other rubbish to contend with. No wonder that in Pompeii, large raised blocks of stone were placed at intervals in the streets to act as stepping-stones for people wishing to cross. There is a commonly held view of Roman cleanliness with its bath-houses, aqueducts and sewers; reality may have been very different.

Gardens and orchards must have existed in open spaces between buildings, especially in the centres of insulae. A list of plants grown is available from some towns such as York; most were wild species, some of which may have been cultivated deliberately for food or medicine, but others were grown and were not always native to Britain. The Romans are said to have introduced many new species (p. 53). The most remarkable evidence for urban gardens comes from Pompeii, where positions of vine-stocks, trees and even vegetables were sealed beneath the debris from Vesuvius in AD 79, showing how British towns may have looked.

But buildings, streets, trees and plants provided only the background for the most important part of urban life: the inhabitants. It is difficult enough to visualize the buildings which once stood below what are now modern towns, or in grass-covered fields, but it is even less easy when we try to repopulate them with a thriving humanity engaged in all its many activities. Once people talked, laughed, shouted and swore, possibly in a variety of languages; children cried, blacksmiths and carpenters hammered, carts rumbled down streets, horses and other animals trod, dogs barked. Direct evidence is obviously difficult to come by for all these aspects of life; nevertheless it exists in the broadest sense, but of varying degree and quality. Apart from sounds, there is another area where it is almost impossible to recreate the local environment: smell, although it has been reproduced at the Jorvik Centre at York. In most towns there was probably an all-pervading atmosphere of unwashed humanity, open cess-pits and earth-closets, and dung. Even in the 1930s, the present writer can remember the universal smell of the latter in the streets of Canterbury, although by then horse transport was in decline.

The activities of the people themselves can often be inferred from their tombstones, since it was the custom in the Roman world to depict scenes from a person's life, or else a family group, and many examples are known from all over the empire. When taken together, it is possible to create a composite picture of urban life. For instance from Ostia come scenes of a tool-merchant and a butcher in their shops, while a blacksmith with his tools is illustrated on a tombstone from York, from where also comes the touching tombstone of a legionary veteran's family, posed almost as formally as a Victorian photograph. But there is a more sinister side to the picture. What was it that carried off at least three and possibly all of the members of this little family at the same time? It is a sombre reminder that the average age of death of all classes at York was about thirty. On a happier note we see the balls in the children's hands, and toys were not uncommon items in the empire; loss or breakage of a favourite will have caused plenty of crying. As for dogs barking, there is the tile from Verulamium showing the footprint of a running dog. Behind it is a pebble embedded in the clay. Obviously the dog had strayed onto the drying tiles, and the stone had been thrown at it. Maybe the dog had yelped in protest. But not all dogs were strays, and many were numbered in the wide range of pets kept by loving owners. A terracotta model from Bordeaux in Gallia Aquitania depicts a cosy domestic scene, with the pet dog lying on the couch across the feet of its master and mistress. Another, from Arlon (Gallia Belgica), shows the adults of a family at table, sitting upright in the Gaulish fashion, and not reclining, while in the scene below, five children cluster round a stewpot; one restrains an over-eager pet dog. Parrots were kept, while the bones of Barbary apes have been found in several places in northern Europe; they were clearly imported as pets.

But as in modern times when pets are often associated with the transmission of disease, so disease and other morbid conditions carried by them or by other agents were very much part of the contemporary environment in the Roman world; with the gross aggregations of populations close together in towns and free movement between them and throughout the empire, disease could very easily reach epidemic proportions and frequently did. Several severe epidemics were brought back to Europe by soldiers returning from eastern campaigns. Human and animal excreta have been found in excavations and must have contributed to their spread and to the general odour emanating from most urban sites. Jars were often placed at street corners for the convenience of passers-by; they were operated by the fullers, who collected human urine for degreasing wool, and this despite large public lavatories in towns, usually connected to the bath-houses and flushed by surplus water from the aqueducts. Yet the semblance of hygiene provided by such services was, in many cases, little more than skin deep, and elsewhere wells are found dug close to sources of contamination. Even in the cooler climates of the north-western empire, flies would have been an abundant nuisance in the summer, carrying disease from place to place. A ditch at Catterick, filled with decaying organic matter, was covered by myriad fly pupa cases (fig. 33), reminding us inexorably of conditions found today in primitive societies. It is not surprising, therefore, that eye disease was particularly prevalent. A not-infrequent article from excavations relating to medical practice is the so-called optician's stamp, inscribed on soft stone and used for imprinting prescriptions on cakes of ointment, all of which were used for treating different eye conditions. Strangely most of these stamps are found in north-western Europe, although the reason for this distribution is not entirely clear; a far higher incidence of eye trouble might have been expected in the eastern provinces, where even now it is endemic. But it may be that some other method, or a different material, which has left no evidence, was used for marking the prescriptions.

There were outbreaks of other major epidemics, coupled with high mortality, recorded in the literature and some of these may have reached Britain. Bubonic plague was

Figure 33 A Flavian-Trajanic ditch filling at Catterick covered in fly pupae cases. Although they are black, reflected light had caused them to show as white, stick-like objects. Scale in inches.

endemic in some parts of the empire, while symptoms akin to smallpox and scarlet fever, linked with severe pulmonary complications, have also been described. It used to be thought that the black rat, a vector of plague, did not occur in Britain until the Norman conquest, yet skeletal material has now been discovered in a well at York; once nobody thought that fleas, another vector of plague, would survive in excavations, but parts of several have recently been found in Roman deposits also at York, together with lice, another carrier of disease, while a bed-bug has been found at Alcester (Warks.). So ultimately we may have proof of such disorders.

Death in childbirth must have been common, as is demonstrated by the gypsum burial of a mother and baby at York. A haematite amulet to protect the wearer from gynaecological disorders came from the villa at Lockleys (Herts.); it contained a Greek palindrome used in invocations to Typhon, an elemental force, Egyptian deities and uterine symbols. Gout was another disease that has been recognized in Britain, in two recorded cases in a large, late Roman cemetery near the amphitheatre at Cirencester (fig. 34); they are the only cases so far identified in the western provinces. Apparently the incidence of the disease has always been high in the Cotswolds, although the reason is not fully understood. But it may explain why *Colchicum autumnale* is still relatively common in the wilds of Gloucestershire, and grows in isolated patches in woodland near Chedworth, not far from Cirencester; normally it grows in open fields and these are probably survivors from days before the wood was created. The alkaloid Colchicine and its associated compounds are still used today as a specific remedy for

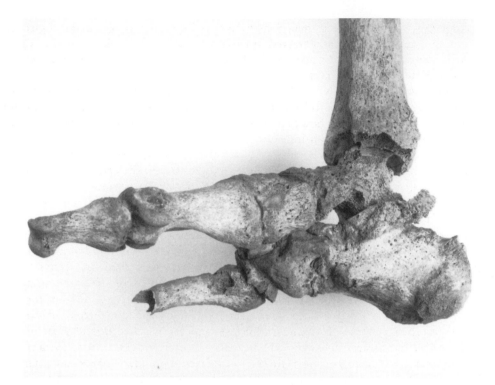

Figure 34 Foot bones from a burial at Cirencester, showing extensive cavitation round the ankle joint due to gout (reproduced by the kind permission of the Corinium Museum and Alan McWhirr).

gout, despite some undesirable side effects. Is there a connexion, or is the distribution of the plant just coincidence? At present, it seems that Colchicum as a remedy for gout was not recognized before the sixth century; before that there may have been some confusion with hellebore, since the foliages are not dissimilar. But it would be interesting to think that a recognized relief for this painful disorder was perhaps first developed in this obscure corner of the Roman Empire.

The maintenance of a complex urban society demands not only a good physical environment, but also the exercise of political functions and the creation of, and respect for, a code of law. There is, of course, much evidence in literary sources for both politics and law in the Roman world, but little of it applies directly to Britain, even if it may have been used. From the less abundant archaeological material there are again some interesting examples, but unfortunately again not much from Britain. Most people are familiar with the election slogans, scratched or painted on walls at Pompeii, but nothing similar occurs in Britain. Nor is there anything to match the address of the emperor Claudius to the Roman Senate, recorded verbatim by the grateful citizens of Gaul on sheets of bronze and erected in their sanctuary at Lyon. In it he pleads that certain citizens of Gallia Comata should be made eligible for magistracies and adlection to the Senate. It is a remarkable piece of political oration. Claudius was aware that there was little sympathy for his proposal among the assembled senators. He was no great orator and did not possess the ability for the eloquent or forceful persuasion of his listeners. So he adopted another expedient beloved of some politicians and bored his audience with an interminable review of Rome's constitutional history from the earliest times onwards, citing case after case in support of his proposal. At one point he hesitated and lost his way; all is recorded and in the end he won his case.

In law, as in politics, much is known, but little of any importance comes directly from Britain. However, the same laws as elsewhere must have applied at least to the coloniae if not to other towns. Therefore it is perfectly justifiable to quote from a cache of bronze plates found in south-eastern Spain. One set gives the legal code which applied to the colonia of Urso (modern Osuna), and regulated, from its foundation, the legal and constitutional administration of the city. It records in detail the duties of the magistrates and council members, methods of holding elections, the setting up of judicial bodies, swearing in of witnesses and other closely related matters for the ordered running of the community. The existence of laws, though, carries with it the immediate corollary of law-breaking and crime, and the whole range of what would now be called 'anti-social behaviour'. Here we have direct evidence from Britain and two examples come from Leicester. In the fourth century a glass-maker, occupying a workshop in the market hall (a major public building in the town centre), spent some of his time melting down in his furnace the base silver coinage of the day to recover the small precious metal content (fig. 35). It was an offence punishable by death as the Codex Theodosianus tells us and yet here he was doing it apparently quite openly in the town centre. The penalty was probably judged by law officers and people alike as too severe for the offence, as in the eighteenth and nineteenth centuries when juries often scaled down the value of a theft to save the neck of some poor unfortunate individual. But long before our criminally minded glass-worker, and in the late second century, an elegant house had stood on the same site, and had contained some high-quality murals. For a time, just before the house was pulled down, it stood vacant and roofless. In this state it became the target of senseless urban vandalism. Damage (fig. 36) was inflicted to the best features of the murals, while graffiti, some obscene, were scratched on the walls; some mention the more bizarre forms of unnatural sexual practices.

When entering these areas of human behaviour, we are beginning to come very close to what has been called the archaeology of the mind. The suggestion is that by careful study and the use of ethnographic models, it is possible to deduce, from the way people acted, what they actually thought in antiquity. This is obviously a major element in any attempts to reconstruct the human environment, which reaches its greatest complexity in urban contexts, but it is also a most dangerous area in which to work, since it requires the exercise of a strictly controlled imagination. Probably the most important aspect here is that which covers religious and superstitious thoughts, since they penetrated equally through every class of society. People have always been superstitious creatures; the more they are at odds with their environment, and the less control they feel they have over it, the greater their belief in supernatural powers. To emphasize this, there is the story of a ring.

Figure 35 A glass furnace in the market hall at Leicester, which had also been used for the illegal extraction of silver from base coinage.

Figure 36 A wall painting from Leicester, which had been extensively damaged by vandals after the house had been left a roofless shell.

Figure 37 A gold finger ring from Silchester bearing the inscription: 'Senicianus, may you live in God' (reproduced by the kind permission of the Haverfield Bequest).

A gold finger ring engraved with a named head of Venus was found in ploughing at Silchester during the eighteenth century (fig. 37). Scratched on it is a secondary inscription which reads: 'May thou live in God, Senicianus', a form of words normally associated with early Christianity; it is interesting that Silchester possesses one of the few possible churches so far identified in Roman Britain. Senicianus is not a very common name in Britain, although it is said to occur frequently in Celtic provinces. It is included in a list of brickmakers from Binchester (Durham) and is mentioned twice on two different curses from Bath (fig. 38). Curses like this were quite common in the Roman world, being used by people to invoke the power of a particular deity – in this case the goddess Sulis – to afflict some malefactor, who had wronged them, with some disease or injury. Some are positively vindictive in their nastiness. Springs were especially sacred to the Roman mind, and the tradition of making offerings to the deity has persisted to the present day. Even as recently as the early nineteenth century, a Welsh clergyman denounced the practice of 'ill-wishing' people by dropping objects into wells in their name. The two Bath curses, although they are written in two different scripts, probably of different dates, both refer to the theft of six silver coins; it would be something of a coincidence to couple twice both the name of a possible thief with an identical crime unless they referred to the same event, even if some lapse of time separated the execution of the curses. The fourth mention of the name is on a curse from Lydney (Glos.) (fig. 39), where in the third century a shrine to the Celtic god Nodens was erected in a long disused hillfort; in addition to the temple of the cult there was a large guest-house complete with a bath suite, a range of single rooms facing the temple, and a good water supply. Nodens' particular powers seem to have been connected with healing and finding. The curse reads:

> To the god, Nodens, Silvianus has lost a ring, he promises half of its value to Nodens. Let him not grant health among those named Senicianus, until he brings it back to the temple of Nodens.

Then again the sinister invocation 'curse renewed'.

Now it is very difficult to avoid the conclusion that the Silchester ring and the Lydney curse were in some way connected. Bath-house petty thieves (*fures balnearii*)

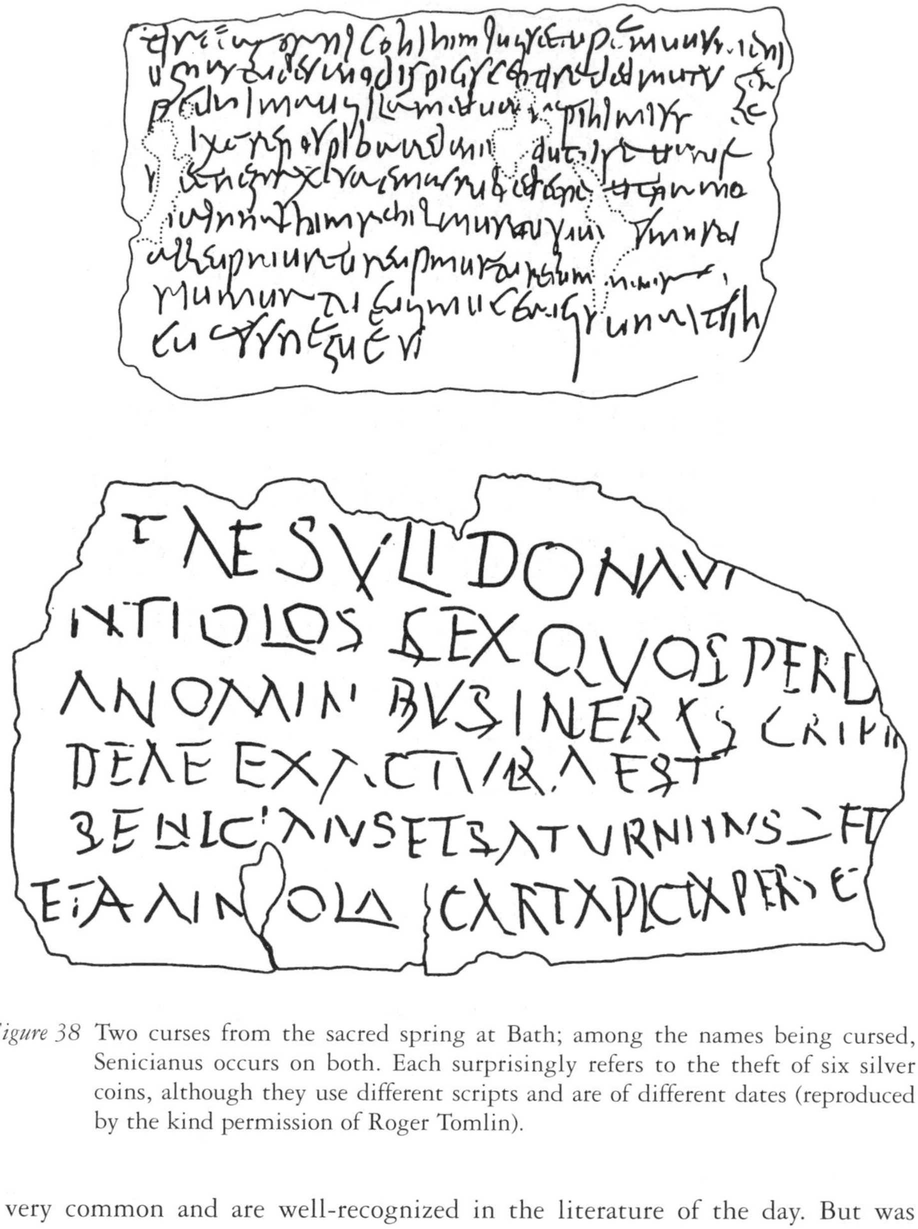

Figure 38 Two curses from the sacred spring at Bath; among the names being cursed, Senicianus occurs on both. Each surprisingly refers to the theft of six silver coins, although they use different scripts and are of different dates (reproduced by the kind permission of Roger Tomlin).

were very common and are well-recognized in the literature of the day. But was Senicianus not just a common thief but a seeker of better health at the temple of Nodens, along with Silvianus, from where he made off with the latter's gold ring? Did he not find a cure at Lydney and therefore stopped at Bath to try his luck with Sulis? By crossing the Severn by ferry, Bath is on the route to Silchester, where he lost the ring. Perhaps he converted to Christianity, with the appropriate inscription being added to the ring hoping that his health would improve after failures with both Nodens and Sulis. It is odd that one of the curses from Bath specifically mentions 'whether Pagan or Christian'. Perhaps the curse worked; primitive, superstitious

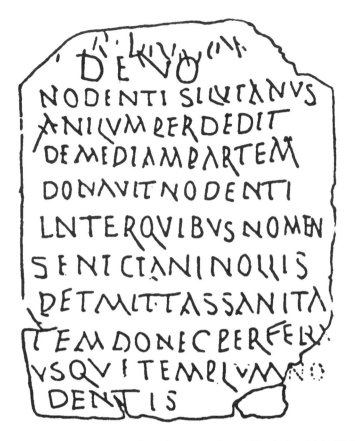

Figure 39 A curse from the temple of Nodens at Lydney (Glos.), in which Silvianus refers to the theft of a ring, with the clear implication that Senicianus was the thief (reproduced by the kind permission of the Haverfield Bequest).

people are highly susceptible to such things, like the 'singing' of Australian aborigines. Nevertheless, Silvianus never recovered the ring, hence the need for 'curse renewed', presumably inscribed on a later visit to Lydney.

This is all, of course, entirely conjectural, but it is possible to weave a fascinating story, which may not be so far from the truth. We shall never know the full history of the ring and the curses, nor the circumstances in which the two protagonists spent their lives, but for one short moment they stand revealed as real people in all their human strengths and weaknesses, with their hopes and fears, ambitions and failures, exposed and illuminated by simple archaeological enquiry.

7

MINERAL EXTRACTION

Mineral extraction has taken place since prehistoric times for a variety of products, but on what must have been a comparatively small scale. It was much enhanced during the Roman period, although most of the working was still confined to the surface. Ores of the main metals such as gold, silver, lead, tin, copper and iron were worked, as were the materials required by the construction industry such as stone, chalk and flint, gravel, sand and clay; moreover much clay was consumed by the pottery, brick and tile industries. All these activities must have resulted in many millions of tonnes being removed from the ground in many parts of the country. Yet it is surprising how little evidence remains. One reason for the lack of survival was caused by later re-working. The Romans were remarkably successful in locating the best quality materials, so much so that they were often followed by medieval and modern man who unfortunately destroyed or confused the earlier evidence.

Most metal ores came from surface workings, so the effect on the landscape was little different from other types of quarrying. However, deeper mines and adits were used in some places. Gold was extracted from extensive surface deposits at Dolaucothi in Carmarthenshire, the only place where it was known to be found in Roman Britain (fig. 40). But the veins of ore were followed underground in a series of shafts, adits and tortuous galleries, kept free of water by a succession of water-lifting wheels, and often followed with a considerable accuracy. The quarries are still visible today on the surface, although they were enlarged in later times, most recently in the 1930s, when a new shaft was sunk to 150 m.

The Roman mines at Dolaucothi are probably the best preserved and investigated in Britain, despite the disturbance by the later works. Today the central area is cloaked in woodland, which somewhat obscures an overall view. But in Roman times it presented a very different appearance. Roman interest was probably stimulated by knowledge of prehistoric placer deposits in the nearby stream beds, exploitation of which was likely to have been continued, so in time revealing the white veins of gold-bearing quartz. A small auxiliary fort was established towards the end of the first century across the river Cothi and under the modern village of Pumsaint; it had been abandoned by the middle of the second century. The presence of a garrison was presumably to protect and control the gold mines, which would have become imperial property. We do not know the nature of its garrison or its name, but it is of interest that the next fort some 15 km further north at Llanio was occupied sometime in the early second century by the *cohors II Asturum*. This regiment had been raised in north-west Spain, where lay the large gold deposits of the province of Tarraconensis and one of the major resources of

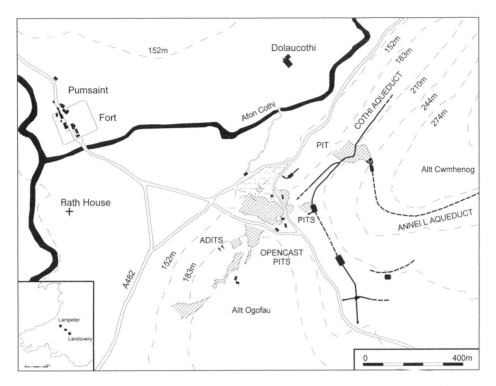

Figure 40 Plan of the gold mining areas and the fort at Dolaucothi (reproduced by the kind permission of Barry Burnham).

the empire. It may well have contained among its personnel those knowledgeable in mining and treating the ores, and its presence near Dolaucothi may have been no accident; indeed a detachment of this regiment may have been stationed at Pumsaint, since the Vindolanda Tablets have shown that troops were often seconded away from their base.

As already stated, the Roman exploitation may have begun with the placer deposits in the river valley. Very soon, however, they must have located the main ore veins which dip below ground level to the south-west at an angle of approximately 35°. It led to working of those deposits near the surface and so resulted in the main quarry areas (fig. 41). This work could be aided by the provision of water in quantity at a higher level by a process known as hushing, which involved the storing of a large volume of water, perhaps as much as a million litres, in a tank at the top of a slope; the water was then released down the slope, so carrying away vegetation, topsoil or other debris to reveal the ore veins. At least two aqueducts are known at Dolaucothi drawing water upstream from both the rivers Cothi and Annell, and then running in contoured channels along the hillside until they arrived above the mining sites, where the water was distributed between a number of tanks. Running water was also needed to recover the gold from the crushed ore. This was done either by panning in wooden cradles, or, for larger quantities of ore, by constructing a series of stepped artificial gullies controlled by sluice gates; branches of gorse or fleeces were often laid across the flow to trap the particles of gold, which was then recovered by burning off the holding material.

Figure 41 Adit entrance to the gold mine at Dolaucothi. It probably represents a later enlargement of possibly original Roman work.

The surface veins were at first followed along their lines, resulting today in a number of narrow cuts still visible in the rocks. As the veins dipped below the surface, adits were formed to extract the ore from underground. These led to galleries and shafts, which have only been partly explored; the depth of the Roman workings is not known. Most of the work was done by hand with pick, wedges and hammers, but fire-setting may also have been employed, in which a fire was started against the rock face to be mined. When thoroughly hot, water was thrown against the face, which caused it to fracture and shatter. Although suitable for surface working, it was somewhat hazardous underground owing to the carbon monoxide and dioxide created by the fire. The air in mines is recorded as often being foul, since ventilation shafts were seldom employed; these gases would have made it lethal, but since the labour was supplied by convicts and slaves, there was probably no shortage of replacements for casualties.

Connected with the mine was a settlement which has yet to be fully explored, but associated burials have been discovered from time to time. There was also a bath-house situated in a loop of the river Cothi, but on the other side from the fort at Pumsaint; whether it was intended for miners or for the garrison is not known, but the management of a bath-house is specifically mentioned in the regulations governing the imperial mines at Vipasca in Spain, so it may have been for the former. Somewhere also must have been the house and offices of a procurator managing the mines.

At its height, probably during the early second century, the mining area must have represented a hive of activity, with perhaps several hundred people employed. It would also have appeared as a bleak and inhospitable landscape, with the exposure of a good deal of bare rock and large mounds of waste, although disused parts would gradually have become covered with annual vegetation and later with scrub as well. There must also have been a level space for crushing and preparing the ore, which was mostly done by hand, using hammers and querns. There is, however, some evidence that mechanically driven wheels were also used for grinding the ore, although the employment of water-powered trip stamps seems to belong to the medieval period. A series of leats, either artificially constructed or natural, carried running water, which was then used for separating the gold from the crushed ore. Nearby were the huts of workers, but it is likely that many of the miners lived permanently underground. Somewhere also must be the places where the extracted gold was smelted and refined and finally cast into ingots. A pall of smoke probably covered the whole area from the fire-setting, many furnaces, domestic hearths, the bath-house and the fort. Fires meant fuel and this was presumably obtained by local coppicing and felling, leading to even more denuding of the local landscape. Much would have been required.

Limited amounts of gold may have been extracted by streaming the rivers of Devon and Cornwall and Scotland, although no proof has yet been found, since these activities would leave little trace. But certain rivers in the former area were streamed for tin, and the gold might have been a by-product in some cases. It is interesting that though the metal is found today in workable quantities in parts of Devon, none occurs in the related river systems, suggesting that most of this source had been worked out some time in antiquity. But this activity would have little effect on the countryside and never seems to have given rise to specialized settlements as at Dolaucothi.

The ground of much of the tin-bearing ores of Cornwall is covered with pits and trenches of the 'old men' which represent attempts to extract the ores in undated antiquity. But tin ingots of the Roman period have been found at St Just and Carnanton, while pewter, an alloy of tin and lead, became quite commonly used for tableware in the fourth century. The only known villa in west Cornwall, at Illogan near Camborne, lying as it does close to the Red River, which was a major source for tin streaming, may have been the result of trying to put the industry onto a more regular footing, with a decent house for a manager or official. It is known that, from the middle of the third century, there was road-building in this area, which may have accompanied renewed government interest in Cornish tin, following the decline of the Spanish mines. The new roads, striking across the landscape, would have been one of the more visible features, with their straight lines and upstanding milestones.

Other metal ores that were extracted and worked in Britain included copper, lead, silver and iron.

Copper ores occur chiefly in north Wales and the Marches. Cakes of the metal have been found in Caernarvonshire and miners appear to have lived in caves at Great Ormes Head during the third and fourth centuries; other cakes come from Anglesey. But there is little trace of the mining activities or of the smelting of the ores, and it is usually assumed that this was organized as a local village activity; there was a minimal impact on the landscape. Rather more evidence comes from Llanymynech (Shropshire), where a mine was entered through a cave from which three galleries radiated. One of these followed the main ore vein for nearly 300 m, and then branched out into smaller galleries and shafts. The miners again appear to have lived in the cave, and once more the impact on the countryside seems to have been minimal, although a certain amount of deforestation must have taken place at all three sites to provide fuel for smelting. Copper is also found in the south-west, but usually as deep deposits which were not worked during the Roman period. However, it may have occurred as placer deposits, and been worked alongside tin, but there is no evidence for specific extraction.

If copper ores were worked as a local, unorganized activity, the mining of lead and silver was a very different matter. The small amount of silver in these ores, which usually occur together, was important to the imperial government, who required it for coinage. Consequently, most of the mines were begun under imperial control and, like those producing gold at Dolaucothi, were better managed. At first military detachments ran the mines, but later they were leased out to concessionaires, such as C. Nipius Ascanius who was working first in Somerset and later in Flintshire, or the Societas Lutudarensis, a company engaged in the Peak District of Derbyshire.

The first ore field to be developed was that in the Mendips of Somerset, where work began only a year or two after the conquest. There grew up a considerable settlement at Charterhouse, which developed around a small fort, and which was sited close to the mines.

As at Dolaucothi, the disturbed countryside was considerable. An area about 1.5 km sq. was ultimately involved, but also, as at that site, later exploitation has masked some of the original Roman work. Several vertically sided trenches up to 5 m deep, south-east of the fort, have been tentatively ascribed to the Roman period, and a dam above the fort to the north-east is also thought to be Roman. This presumably retained water used possibly for hushing, for washing the ore, and it may also have supplied a bath-house. Well-made drains (or water channels?) are the only sign so far of water being conducted round the site. The main settlement grew up north of the fort and an irregular grid of streets can be seen on aerial photographs, with a small amphitheatre situated some distance away to the west. The latter seems never to have been provided with masonry walls. In most respects, therefore, the settlement resembled a small town and would have possessed very similar features of form, texture and colour. The only major difference would have been the many smelting furnaces, mostly situated in the open or in rough shacks, not only because of the fire risk, but also because of the highly poisonous nature of the lead fumes, which required good ventilation. Lead poisoning was a recognized complaint in the Roman world, although little enough seems to have been done about it; convicts and slaves were cheap. The lead and silver were separated in cupelling furnaces, lined with bone ash and most likely fuelled with charcoal. Charcoal burning contributed yet more smoke. Coupled with the smell of burning flesh and bones from the production of bone ash, and added to the other fumes pervading the area, together with odourless but poisonous carbon monoxide, and combined with the general bleakness of the site, a most unpleasant and unhealthy working environment was probably created. One is reminded inexorably of the sites of the early industrial revolution and the Black Country.

Other places that produced lead and silver ores were in the Peak District of Derbyshire, where the Societas Lutudarensis held sway, in Flintshire on the Welsh borders, and, to a lesser extent, in Yorkshire, Shropshire and some other counties in the Pennines.

The Derbyshire mines were large-scale producers of lead with a low silver content and seem at first to have been centred around the fort at Brough-on-Noe. It is not known how the mines were organized, although a small settlement grew up at Carsington not far away, in which case, it has been suggested, the ores would have been collected from a number of mines in the area and taken to the centre for smelting. The same dispersal of effort appears to have been employed in Flintshire, where the ores from the mines in the Halkyn Mountains were collected and taken first to Flint for smelting and then to Pentre on the river Dee for making up into finished goods. The main ore vein here occurs at a height of 300 m on the north-west scarp of the carboniferous limestone of the mountain, and was worked by trenching, the scars of which still remain. The dispersal of the industry would have caused less disruption of the landscape, although the main centres of activity would, as at Charterhouse, have been blighted. A site more similar to Charterhouse is at Linley in Shropshire. There the mining of the hillside seems to have been aided by hushing, for holding tanks and an aqueduct have been identified. The main smelting centre seems to have been about a kilometre to the south-west.

Of all the metals found in Britain, probably the most important, if not the most valuable, was iron, which has a wide distribution in nature. Principal areas where it is found were the Weald of Kent and Sussex and the Forest of Dean, while varying quantities occur along the Jurassic Ridge, particularly in Northamptonshire. Other smaller areas were in Cumbria and Northumberland. Iron deposits were also found as workable strata in the clays of Norfolk, and at Wanborough (Wilts.).

The Weald was a heavily forested area in antiquity. During the Roman period there was little evidence of permanent settlement, although it was crossed by four main roads. One of these roads was surfaced, throughout its course through the Weald, with iron slag, readily acquired from the smelting works. Indeed, most of the evidence for iron-working in this area is obtained from the giant slag heaps, often covering several hectares of ground and several metres high. The ore fields were based on the Wadhurst Clays and divided roughly into two areas: one near the coast behind Hastings, the other further inland and more centrally placed. Tiles stamped with the mark of *Classis Britannica* have been found associated with some of the sites and probably the fleet ran its own iron industry, which, when coupled with the excellent timber supplies of the same area, provided for most of its basic needs. One of the sites, which has produced a large number of stamped tiles, was at Beauport Park, near Battle, and covered over 5 ha. It was chiefly noted for its remarkable slag heaps, which it has been calculated originally contained upwards of 100,000 tonnes; much of it was extracted for road-building during the nineteenth century. The settlement, although primarily industrial, also contained a residential area and a bath-house. Apart from the latter, most buildings were timber-framed with walls of wattle-and-daub, although masonry structures must have existed. The visual appearance would again have been not unlike a minor town.

A similar, but slightly smaller settlement existed further inland at Bardown, near Wadhurst. Here, evidence for mining was found in numerous pits extending for at least 2 km away from the site, which was itself divided into two parts: one industrial and the other residential. A side-line seems to have been the manufacture of pottery and tiles. Again, as at Beauport Park, the placing of the residential area away from the industrial part would appear sensible but for the fact that the latter was to the west; in consequence the former would have been repeatedly covered by smoke, fumes and smuts whenever the wind blew from the west.

It is worth mentioning in this context the Cogidubnus inscription from Chichester. This was dedicated by a *collegium fabrorum*, which has been variously interpreted as a guild of blacksmiths or shipwrights. Whatever their nature, they would undoubtedly have been using Wealden iron, showing the distance it travelled.

The Forest of Dean lies mainly on a ridge of carboniferous limestone, between the Old Red Sandstone of south-east Wales and the west bank of the river Severn. It contains bands of variable thickness of ferruginous marl, which was the primary source of ore.

While most of the mining was restricted to surface trenching, deeper works have also been found. An adit was excavated during the uncovering of the temple complex at Lydney and was traced into the hillside for over 15 m. Although some of the ore was processed locally, much was shipped, possibly by the rivers Wye and Severn, to outlying sites, such as Weston-under-Penyard and Gloucester. The former was an unfortified town, but the latter was a colonia. Weston-under-Penyard seems to have been a major iron-working centre and one slag heap covered 80 ha. The industry was, therefore, probably more dispersed than the Weald, but the visual appearance would not have been dissimilar, with forest clearings, small, possibly temporary settlements and all the paraphernalia of mining and processing.

Another principal ore field was the ferruginous sand and limestone country of Northamptonshire. Here, work seems to have centred on the two minor towns of Water Newton and Irchester, although many sites have been destroyed by more modern open-cast mining. The remnants of Rockingham Forest cover some of the area, and it is to be assumed that much more was forested in the Roman period. Outlying, more dispersed sites away from the main centres also existed, such as that at Wakerley, where an Iron Age enclosure and hut circles suggest pre-Roman working. The interesting feature of the latter site is that not only was iron worked, but also pottery was made in addition to agricultural activities such as corn drying. Moreover there was an aisled barn, which could have provided housing as well as storage. We seem to have then an industrial settlement which was self-supporting for food, implying that forest cleared for fuel was turned into cultivated fields in which both barley and wheat were grown. The evidence for domestic animals, though, was slight; meat did not feature highly in the diet, although some bones showed knife cuts from butchery. It may be that there was little pasture and livestock farming, and that carcasses were brought to the site when meat was required. It is therefore easier to imagine the visual appearance of Wakerley, which obviously differed from the mining settlements so far considered: a large forest clearing, with coppiced woodland on its fringes; cultivated fields occupying the nearer land, which may have been cleared in the Iron Age, and, at the centre, timber buildings and all the filth associated with an industrial site.

Another difference to be observed in this area is the presence of a number of villas, unlike the other industrial zones already described. Whether any were specifically related to the iron industry cannot be decided, but it is not impossible that it was part of their source of wealth, together with farming.

Water Newton was not only a centre of the iron industry; pottery was also made on a large scale. During the fourth century it became a principal production centre for pottery which was then carried over much of northern and eastern Britain. The chief difference between these sites making pottery and those of the metal industries would have been the large clay pits; unfortunately little is known about them since most research has been concentrated on the manufacturing process, which was spread over a wide area. But the amount of pottery produced in these kilns must have demanded considerable resources. Otherwise the visual appearance would have been very similar

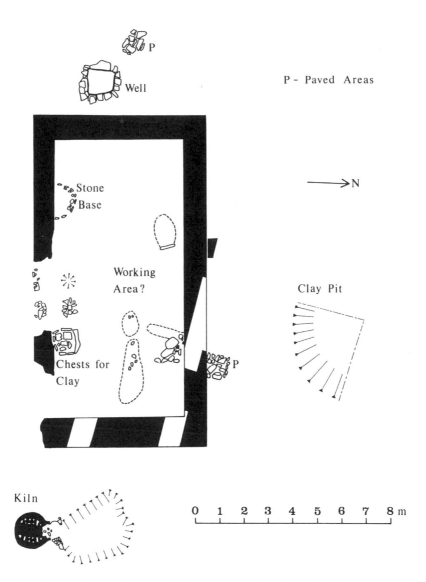

Figure 42 A potter's workshop at Stibbington, near Peterborough. Close to the building were situated a well, a clay pit and a kiln.

to any other industrial area, with rudimentary workshops, mostly built of timber, levelled places, with perhaps some covering, where the finished pots could be dried before firing, and the kilns themselves. A small kiln could accommodate upwards of 200 average-sized vessels, and some were appreciably bigger. A typical factory has been found at Stibbington, near Water Newton (fig. 42). Here a rectangular building, with masonry foundations, and perhaps half-timbered, contained a working area and a chest for prepared clay; outside lay a well, the kiln and a clay pit. Nothing else was needed except fuel, which was probably gathered by local coppicing. Such a factory could produce several hundred pots from each firing.

Production of pottery, bricks or tiles requires only three raw materials: clay, water and fuel. Additionally it has to be close to a transport system, preferably by water, which was the safest way to carry heavy, bulky and fragile goods, if the finished products were to be distributed over a wide area. Thus many industrial areas were set up at one time or another in the Roman period, often close to rivers or the coast.

The industry based at Water Newton on the river Nene was also well placed to use the main road system. Other places of production were Colchester, where its position on the river Colne was only a short distance from the sea; Oxfordshire was well placed for the river Thames and also main roads; Mancetter-Hartshill (Warks.) was close to the sources of three of the main river systems of Britain, the Severn, Trent and Nene; Purbeck (Dorset) not only was near the coast, but was also close to a good harbour at Poole; Crambeck (N. Yorks.) was near the river Derwent. There were many more besides this selection. Indeed, wherever suitable raw materials were to be found, pots could be made, and not all kilns were at the centres of large industrial areas; isolated kilns could provide for purely local needs.

In contrast, there seem to have been few similar sites devoted to bricks and tiles, which were mostly made to satisfy local demand. However, one site at Minety (Wilts.), not far from Cirencester, seems to have been producing large quantities, stamped with the initials of the manufacturer. There was also a municipal brickworks near Gloucester. But brick and tile kilns, although larger than pottery kilns, were of a very temporary nature, and were almost entirely situated above ground; consequently they leave little trace of their existence. Presumably they were large clamp-like structures, with the green tiles stacked on the open ground and covered with straw and clay; vents would be left in the sides and top for the fires.

Another industry which often gave rise to its own settlements was salt production, the extraction of which may have been an imperial monopoly. Salt works were mostly situated in low-lying coastal regions, such as the estuaries of the Thames, Severn, Dee and Wash, but there were also at least two inland places at Droitwich and Middlewich, which were both given the Roman name *Salinae*, and where salt was extracted from saline springs rising from the ground. These gave rise to two small towns, which, with their heavy industrial accent, will have resembled in appearance other similar centres like Charterhouse. The environment may have been slightly cleaner and they would lack the characteristic features of the slag heaps, but they would still have contained many furnaces for evaporating the brine in shallow pans of lead or clay, so polluting the atmosphere with their smoke and fumes. Some waste tips of broken clay pans and furnace linings have been found.

The latter were the main features of the sites situated near the coasts, forming great mounds of fire-reddened debris and giving rise to the so-called Red Hills of Essex. The organization of these sites seems to have been more lax and dispersed and can have caused only transient, rudimentary settlements; but we need not doubt the controlling hand of Rome in the background, for the level of production was greatly in excess of local needs. Indeed, connexions have been suggested between the main salt-producing areas and the major centres of the pottery industry, which may have produced containers for the salt. Thus Colchester lay near the Essex coast; Upchurch in Kent could have served the Thames estuary; Nene Valley wares could have provided containers for the Fens; and the Severn valley kilns, near Droitwich, produced similar vessels.

The building trades required large quantities of stone and mineral aggregates, for roads as well as structures. Unfortunately, as in the mining industry, many Roman quarries provided the starting points for medieval and modern working, with the result that most of the earlier evidence has been removed. But some quarries have survived and, moreover, there is information recorded from earlier years in places now destroyed by modern workings. Needless to say, most quarries of the Roman period would have considerably altered the local landscape, and reference has been made to those near Inchtuthil (p. 34).

Some of the most noteworthy examples are found in the region of Hadrian's Wall. Had this frontier work been completed at its full width of 3 m, over 1.5 million m³ of masonry would have been required, which gives some idea of the scale of operations. Even with the reduction in width westwards from the river Irthing, and the replacement of lime mortar with puddled clay in some sections, well over 0.5 million m³ of stone were used. Moreover, clay and sand had to be dug and limestone quarried for mortar. With all these quarries and pits, a wide strip of countryside must at first have been reduced to something resembling a lunar landscape. Some of the quarries providing the stone have been identified, mainly producing carboniferous limestone, but with sandstone lying west of the Red Rock fault, near the river Irthing. They occasionally carry inscriptions cut on the surviving rock faces recording the men and units working them. Such a one is the 'Written Rock' of Gelt, near Brampton, which tells us that a vexillation of Legio II under the *optio* Agricola was working there during the consulships of Aper and Maximus (AD 207). Another of considerable size lies at Bleatarn, while yet another inscription has been found on an ancient quarry face on Fallowfield Fell, near Chollerford. Most have been destroyed by more modern operations, but both quarries and worked outcrops of rock survive best in the higher, central section of the Wall; there they have been identified extending for 800 m south of it. Some were later used as rubbish dumps, while all will in time have become clothed with vegetation, softening the harsh outlines and eventually concealing them.

Other quarries, this time in limestone, have been partly excavated outside Cirencester. A large group was situated under and around the amphitheatre, and was later partly used as a cemetery. It is almost certain that the amphitheatre was built in a disused quarry, with one of the seating banks being placed against the face, while the floor of the arena and its gateways lay over an area which had been levelled with quarry waste. Other quarries outside Cirencester have also been identified north of the town.

Extraction of a very different type of rock took place near Canterbury. During modern working, a Roman chalk pit was broken into, containing a hoard of early fourth-century coins. Chalk was not a satisfactory building stone, although it was used for foundations and internal work; it breaks up badly on exposure to frost. It was therefore being quarried either to extract the flint or to provide material for burning into lime. The quarry must have been opened at about the time when the defences were being built, which would have consumed large quantities of materials during their construction.

Other quarries, both large and small, must have existed wherever good stone outcropped, or was near the surface, close to building sites. But this was not always the case, and stone sometimes had to be carried for considerable distances. The walls of London were dressed with Kentish rag, probably obtained from near Maidstone, while a monumental arch there was made of Lincolnshire limestone. Bath stone and Purbeck marble were both used for tombstones at Colchester, and it is possible that Bath stone was an imperial monopoly; an inscription from a 'villa' at Combe Down, just outside the town, mentions a principia restored by some imperial procurator's assistants and the house could have been the headquarters for these quarries. Purbeck marble was sometimes used for monumental inscriptions and was carried widely over the province. Charnwood slates and granite as well as Derbyshire millstone grit were employed at Leicester. Much of this material could have been carried by water, but the large blocks of the latter stone used in a number of buildings must have been brought by road, since there was no convenient alternative. All these stones, and many others, must have been extracted from quarries which left large scars on the landscape, only healed in time as vegetation grew and covered them after disuse.

Aggregate for road-building was, as with stone, mostly extracted locally, although usually in a series of small pits alongside the road. It is interesting, though, that at both Cirencester and Brough-on-Humber the surfacing material of the internal streets was changed from gravel to limestone quarry waste at about the time when masonry fortifications were built; no doubt there was so much waste that it was cheaper and easier to use. Gravel pits have been found inside the walls at Canterbury, and bordering the Fosse Way at Thorpe-by-Newark and neighbouring Brough. Although at first they would have denuded and scarred the landscape, they were frequently filled with rubbish, and vegetation would have soon smoothed out the appearance. The quantities of material used over the whole Roman period were considerable, since repair consisted of laying a fresh surface of aggregate. This was particularly true in towns where road surfaces often rose as much as 3 m during the Roman period. At Cirencester, for instance, the streets used up to $150,000 \, m^3$ of aggregate, which represented a quarry hole 100 m by 50 m and 30 m deep.

Behind most of these industrial activities there was one common requirement, which probably caused the greatest impact on the countryside: the supply of fuel. Fire-setting, smelting, forging, purifying of metals, firing of pottery, brick and tile, evaporation of brine, drying of cereals, and all other domestic and agricultural processes, such as the heating of bath-houses, cooking, brewing and baking, all required fuel.

Coal was certainly dug from surface deposits, but was not suitable for all purposes, such as the smelting of iron ore because of the sulphur content; but it has been found at over seventy sites of the Roman period, and seems to have been fairly widely used. It was carted, perhaps by water where possible, for considerable distances. The main coalfields ranged from Durham and Northumberland by way of Yorkshire and Derbyshire to the Forest of Dean and Somerset, with some local sites being supplied from south Wales; the Romans, therefore, exploited all the main coalfields of England and Wales with the exception of Staffordshire, and may even have imported some from the Rhineland. Working from outcrops would have produced areas similar to quarries, although the surroundings, including the vegetation, may have become covered in a ubiquitous black dust.

But wood and charcoal must have been the main sources of fuel. Charcoal was fired in clamps from which all air was excluded. Experiments have shown that this could be achieved by cutting, and drying undercover, billets of coppiced wood up to a metre in length. It was stacked radially with a central space for the fire; up to 10 tonnes could

Figure 43 Newly coppiced woodland. On the left an earlier area has partly regenerated after three to four years of growth. In the background is mature coppice nearly ready for cutting.

be carbonized in one firing. When the stack was complete it was covered by vegetation and soil. Once it was burning the top was also sealed and left for three to four days and then extinguished with water; it was only opened when thoroughly cold. It was noted during the experiment that acrid smoke was given off throughout the firing, which, with any number of clamps being used at the same time, must have provided a most unpleasant atmosphere in which to work.

Charcoal-burning even then can only have supplied a small amount of the total fuel consumed. For the larger portion, wood was needed in quantities, and must have resulted in considerable deforestation in those regions near settlements or industrial areas. It could be obtained from several sources. Clearing undergrowth and trimming hedges can provide a certain amount in the form of faggots. Similarly, the felling of large trees for building works always produces some smaller branches, trimmings and off-cuts which are suitable for fuel. There is also some evidence that coppicing was practised in the Roman period, in which the wood is seen as a crop, regenerating over seven to ten years (fig. 43). Most trees are suitable for this treatment, although ash, birch, willow and hazel were perhaps the best species; more recently beech and chestnut have both been used. Woodland management requires parcels always to be ready for felling, while others are in various stages of regeneration. A very large area of woodland is therefore required to keep up a regular supply of firewood over a period of time.

Approximate figures of consumption have been worked out from experiment. Thus for a very small bath-house at the villa at Welwyn (Herts.) a figure of 13 kg/hour has been estimated as the consumption needed to keep the heated rooms 10°C above the outside temperature; this is equivalent to *c*. 114 tonnes per year. It has been suggested that coppiced wood only produces *c.* 5 tonnes/ha, so that to keep the baths hot all the year round would require 20–25 ha. of coppice; there would be little economy gained in lighting the fires only when the baths were required. Suppose the woodland was managed on an eight-year regeneration programme, then a total of 160–200 ha would be needed to keep this one small bath suite, consisting of no more than three heated rooms, supplied with fuel. The same villa also contained an even larger bath-house, about twice the size of the one described here. When this is taken into the calculation, together with the requirements for cooking, other forms of heating, and perhaps industrial processes as well, then we can perhaps envisage an associated woodland area of over 500 ha. With possibly up to 1,000 baths, some larger, some smaller, functioning in Britain at the same time, something like half a million hectares of managed woodland would have been devoted to the sole purpose of keeping the occupants clean and warm!

A unique wooden writing tablet was found in 1986 in the bed of the Walbrook in London, which shows that woodland ownership could be legally registered, carrying with it the implication of management. It is the first 'page' of a legal document, which was much longer, and was presumably executed under judicial authority on 14 March 118, early in Hadrian's reign. It is so far the sole survivor of many such documents which must once have applied to almost all the land of Roman Britain: an equivalent to the modern Land Registry, where land was surveyed and ownership registered. It refers to a dispute over the ownership of a parcel of woodland, called *silvam Verlucionium*, in the *pago Dibussu{ }* of the *civitate Cantiacorum* (modern Kent), measuring about 1.85 ha, which was bought for 40 denarii by Julius Bellicus from Valerius Silvinus. This was not a large sum, but Julius Bellicus was prepared to go to law for it, stressing the importance of the possession of a small parcel of woodland, presumably in the first instance as a source of fuel, a valuable commodity.

Experiments on industrial production have also been carried out, notably on the manufacture of pottery. A small kiln, containing perhaps no more than fifty vessels, consumed around 150–200 kg of dry wood to complete the firing; many kilns could accommodate up to 200 vessels. Green wood weighs as much as a third more than dry wood, so this figure becomes 200–270 kg of freshly coppiced material. Using the figures quoted above, and allowing regeneration at the same rate, it would require nearly 0.75 ha of woodland to keep one small kiln in production. It can be seen, therefore, that domestic and industrial processes would between them have needed many hectares of woodland, the use of which could not but have an extreme effect on the landscape. Although it would not have led to complete deforestation, it must have altered quite considerably the appearance of the countryside, in a way that the construction of single towns, forts and settlements could not.

8

CHANGE IN THE ROMAN PERIOD

The return of a 'natural' landscape

So far little mention has been made of chronology, and it is now necessary to put the subjects dealt with into a chronological framework.

If we start from the premise that a good deal of land had already been cleared for agriculture during the Iron Age, especially in the south-east, then the arrival of the Roman army in AD 43 will have had only a minimal effect on the landscape. The two principal demands would have been cereals and timber. The first was immediate, while the second only grew in the early decades of the conquest as the army began to build fortresses and forts, until by about AD 50 the first phase of installations had been constructed to mark out the boundaries of the new province, which ran approximately along the lines of the river Trent and lower reaches of the Severn, and included a considerable number of vexillation fortresses as well as the fortress at Colchester, which was now abandoned. This frontier was later modified under Ostorius Scapula by pushing the southern half into the Welsh Marches, and by the time of the Boudiccan rebellion in AD 60–1 the army was campaigning in north Wales as far as Anglesey. What we cannot calculate is the quantity of timber that was salvaged for reuse when a fort or fortress was abandoned and a new one established in another place. In this way quite considerable economies could be made, so lessening the amount of new wood which had to be felled. But hand in hand with these military advances went the foundation of new towns to the rear, at London, Colchester, Verulamium, and possibly some sort of nucleated communities at Chichester, Silchester and Canterbury. It is difficult to describe their nature, for military occupation seems to have lingered on at these latter sites for some time beyond the Boudiccan rebellion. So, after the initial spurt of intense activity, demand for timber will have declined, although that for cereals may have increased.

After the Boudiccan rebellion a period of stagnation set in for the next decade. There were, of course, the sacked towns of Verulamium, Colchester and London to be rebuilt, but this did not proceed in a regular fashion but was frequently delayed. Moreover, roads had to be consolidated, which, following the original linear clearances, would have resulted in a good deal of local quarrying for aggregate.

The next phase of major military operations embraced firstly the campaigns of Petillius Cerialis in the early 70s, when he advanced into Brigantia. Although he probably reached as far north as Carlisle, the advance was not followed by the construction of new forts, except in east Yorkshire, where it included the fortress of York, which was now added to the list of similar permanent installations at Gloucester, Wroxeter and Lincoln. The next governor, Julius Frontinus, turned attention again to

Wales, starting two new fortresses at Caerleon and Chester and also a small number of auxiliary forts, but this was matched by the evacuation of some of the forts in the midlands and south-west. This construction will have called for a fair amount of new timber, but again we are left with the insoluble problem of how much timber was salvaged for reuse. It also raises the question of what happened to those areas released from military occupation, which were almost certainly constituted as civitates with their own self-government. From that process began the growth of the second phase of civitas capitals. Work had also begun in the Mendips silver/lead mines, within the first five years of the occupation.

But it was left to Frontinus' successor, Julius Agricola, to round off the conquest of Wales, occupy Brigantia, and initiate the conquest and occupation of Scotland. In the course of six campaigns he finally defeated the Caledonians at Mons Graupius, which can probably be placed near Durno in north-east Scotland, and occupied the area up to the Highland fringe. Moreover, his advance took him beyond the site of the battle and along the east coast plain, where a chain of campaign camps marks his passage, almost as far as the Moray Firth.

During the decade or so covered by the governorships of Frontinus and Agricola, nearly a hundred new forts and fortresses had been built and over 2,000 km of new roads had been established in the newly conquered areas; to provide them with garrisons led to the wholesale evacuation of the lowland zone and the constitution of at least ten new civitates, all of which would require capitals (fig. 44). Moreover the death of the client king, Cogidubnus, at about this time caused the break up of his kingdom and the establishment of at least two more civitates. It is not surprising, therefore, that the Flavian period saw the biggest upheaval in the landscape so far, with even more extensive deforestation, the beginning of large-scale quarrying and mining, and the general start of romanized country buildings; during the Julio-Claudian period the latter had been restricted to those of a few wealthy owners. Also, there would have been a gradual increase in all types of agricultural production to provide for the demands of the Roman tax-collectors, as well as the agriculturally unproductive new towns.

The first withdrawal from Scotland, ultimately to the Tyne–Solway line, in the late years of the first century and early years of the second century, was caused by a number of factors, the chief of which was the reduction in strength of the British garrison. It may have led to a certain amount of local disturbance and a number of forts appear to have been burnt. But this need not have been the result of enemy action. Most of the forts in southern Scotland had been standing for nearly twenty years, and it might be thought that the timbers were rotting and past salvaging; consequently they were burnt by the Roman army. Had that been the case there were implications for the supply of timber.

The withdrawal from Scotland was matched by a consolidation further south, where work began in *c.* AD 100 converting all three legionary fortresses, now at Caerleon, Chester and York, from timber to masonry. It was accompanied by the foundation of two new coloniae in the abandoned fortresses at Lincoln and Gloucester. All this construction will have required large new quarries, which were usually local. But in the new towns there is some indication that economies were being practised in the use of masonry, possibly as a temporary measure. At Lincoln and also in the newly founded civitas capitals at Exeter and Silchester, timber was wholly or partly used for the forum

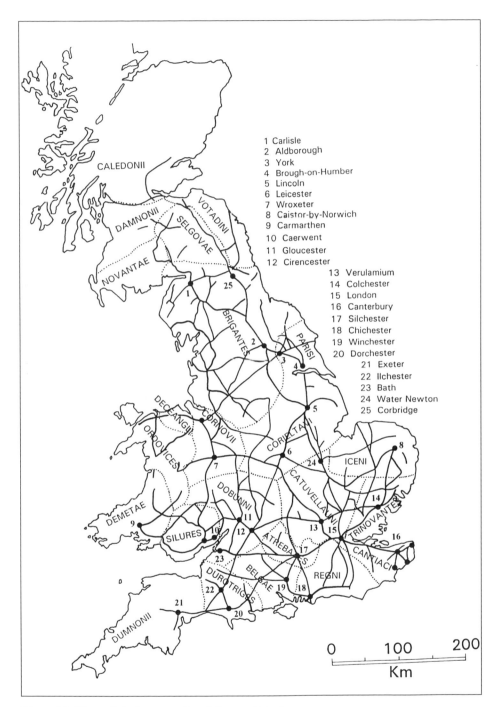

1 Carlisle
2 Aldborough
3 York
4 Brough-on-Humber
5 Lincoln
6 Leicester
7 Wroxeter
8 Caistor-by-Norwich
9 Carmarthen
10 Caerwent
11 Gloucester
12 Cirencester
13 Verulamium
14 Colchester
15 London
16 Canterbury
17 Silchester
18 Chichester
19 Winchester
20 Dorchester
21 Exeter
22 Ilchester
23 Bath
24 Water Newton
25 Corbridge

Figure 44 The political geography of Roman Britain.

and basilica. This is in contrast to the fora at Cirencester and Verulamium, where masonry seems to have been used from the start. Some other towns were not even rich enough to provide timber and had to make do with an open space for a forum for the time being, such as Leicester and possibly Chichester and Wroxeter. Progress in the civitas capitals was fitful.

After the withdrawal from Scotland, there was a brief period when an attempt was made to consolidate a northern frontier on the Solway–Tyne line, which seems to have culminated in a major war at the beginning of Hadrian's principate. It was followed by a visit of the emperor in person.

Hadrian's visit to Britain began a process which was already in being in other provinces: the conversion of defence in depth, typified by the placing of forts at tactical and strategic points throughout an area, to a linear defensive line upon which the garrisons could be concentrated. This change in strategy resulted in the construction of Hadrian's Wall, which, because it separated two warlike tribes in Britain, had to be that much stronger than the German frontier, where a timber palisade had sufficed. The new frontier was, as it were, a fortified line through the middle of potentially hostile territory and had to be prepared to look both ways. As already described, its construction must have had a startling effect on the landscape.

Hadrian died in AD 138 and was succeeded by Antoninus Pius, who rapidly changed the frontier policy, mainly because Hadrian's Wall, although in many ways successful, had created political problems which it was deemed could be solved by advancing the frontier to the old temporary line of Agricola across the Forth–Clyde isthmus and reoccupying the whole of southern Scotland. So the Antonine Wall was constructed, and continued in occupation until a serious Brigantian revolt in *c*. 154–5 resulted in a withdrawal southwards for a short time, during which Hadrian's Wall was recommissioned. Although the Antonine Wall was reoccupied briefly, the strain on the British garrison imposed by this reoccupation, not only of the advanced frontier, but also now of a number of forts in Brigantia, as well as lowland Scotland, was too great. There were simply not enough troops, and no reinforcements could be expected, so the decision was taken by the new emperor, Marcus Aurelius, to withdraw the frontier again to Hadrian's Wall, where, with the exception of some campaigns further north, on several occasions, it remained for the rest of the Roman period.

The provision of garrisons for these new frontiers and their associated forts could only be achieved by the evacuation of those in south Wales and to the east of the Pennines; the Brigantes to the west of the Pennines and in the Lake District were still of too uncertain loyalty to be relieved of military control. As a result several new civitates were constituted, as had happened in the Flavian period, but this time they did not give rise to large capitals; only Caerwent, in the territory of the Silures, although small, seems to have been built along standard lines. But both Carmarthen and Aldborough, capitals of the Demetae and Brigantes respectively, if they were better known, may yet turn out to resemble them. Brough-on-Humber, on the other hand, if it was not still a naval base, did not, even though it possessed a theatre, which was most likely connected with a religious establishment.

By then also, most of the civitas capitals in the south had fully developed. Most of the major public buildings had been completed by the Antonine period: the masonry forum at Silchester by *c*. AD 100, the Wroxeter forum by 130 and those at Leicester and Caistor-by-Norwich by the middle of the century. London may have had an earlier, smaller forum, which was completely rebuilt on a much larger scale at the beginning of the second century. At Cirencester, the first basilica was built on unstable ground and had to be rebuilt towards the middle of the second century. Most of the towns had bath-houses and amphitheatres and the occasional theatre had been provided. Masonry was mostly employed for public buildings, but many houses and shops were still constructed about timber frames or half-timbering on dwarf walls, so that although requirements for stone activated more quarries, there remained a demand for good structural timber. Sometimes, as at Leicester, Verulamium or London, walls were built with puddled clay, or unbaked clay bricks, thus alleviating the need for high-quality stone, which was not present locally.

The demand for food and other agricultural produce caused by these towns and an increased garrison was also making great changes to the countryside. The maximum area under cultivation during the Roman period had probably not yet been reached, but it must have increased considerably over that which was available in the first century. Moreover the villa system can be discerned with its owner-occupier, landlord-tenant, small-holder and residual native farmer relationships, although in the majority of cases in Britain it is impossible to be precise about them. But the beginnings of some of the large landed estates, which emerged in the fourth century, must have been started. This expansion was aided by technical improvements in agricultural machinery and by better transport, which enabled produce to be marketed more easily. Land could be cleared and cultivated, woods managed and crops and stocks improved by careful selective breeding.

The last decades of the second century saw much unrest on the northern frontier and possibly also in Wales, which culminated, after the assassination of the emperor Commodus in AD 192, in a major war. The governor, Clodius Albinus, was hailed as one of four rivals in the succession, but with only four legions at his disposal was no match for the sixteen commanded by Septimius Severus on the Rhine and Danube. In 197, Albinus collected his troops and crossed to Gaul, where he was defeated at Lyon by the superior strength of Severus. In the absence of most of the British garrison, there was an invasion by the Maeatae and Caledonians from Scotland and another rebellion of the Brigantes. No doubt seeing the empty forts, they seized the opportunity, thinking that Rome had departed for good, and there was much destruction of military works.

Severus, however, had other ideas, and in the same year sent a loyal follower to be procurator of Britain, followed by a succession of able governors. However, his plans took him over a decade, and his own presence in Britain, without reaching a successful conclusion; he died at York leaving the final settlement to his son Caracalla. Nevertheless he campaigned as far as the Highlands, possibly envisaging a reoccupation of Scotland.

The rest of Britain did not escape punishment. Supporters of Albinus were hunted out, their land was often sequestered, and the villas at Ditchley and Lullingstone, among others, show a period of abandonment at this time. What happened then is difficult to judge; presumably they first became imperial estates, but that was not necessarily the end of the matter. They might have been managed by a procurator's assistant, or sold, or given to some favoured supporter. Worst of all, the associated land might have been left vacant, perhaps reverting to nature, which can happen quite quickly in only a few years; the change on the landscape would then have been more dramatic.

The last decades of the second century also saw a fundamental alteration in the urban landscape with the construction of earthwork defences around many major and minor towns. They normally took the form of an earth bank of dump construction with a ditch, or sometimes two, in front of it. There is a suggestion from one or two places that these were accompanied by internal interval-towers of timber, and possibly also of timber gates, but in most cases they seem to have been built in conjunction with masonry gates, sometimes of monumental proportions, as at Cirencester.

The third century was a time of upheaval in the whole empire, from which Britain, although largely isolated from the main events, did not entirely escape, especially from the rampant inflation which came with it. It also saw the start of a great programme of construction of masonry urban fortifications, beginning with London, probably in the late second century, and ending with the minor towns of Catterick and Thorpe, which were not finished until the early fourth century. Large quantities of stone were required for this work and numerous quarries were presumably begun or extended. Sometimes they were some distance from the towns where the stone was being used and transport was, where feasible, by water. Thus at London, a ship carrying a cargo of Kentish ragstone from near Maidstone sank in the dock and was not salvaged.

Throughout this period, the northern frontier remained peaceful after the settlement of Caracalla. It is likely that the British garrison was reduced in strength by the despatch of legionary vexillations to the Continent soon after the middle of the century. They were accompanied by a number of auxiliary regiments, but none ever returned, since by then Britain had become part of the breakaway Gallic Empire of Postumus. The overall picture is confused and it is not entirely known how these troop movements affected the forts in the north. There is disputed evidence for abandonment in some, possibly at Birdoswald, Halton and Rudchester, yet the outpost forts seem to have been held, often with enhanced garrisons, together with many of the forts south of the frontier.

But what is not in dispute is the growth of civil settlements outside the occupied forts during the third century. For these vici, it was a period of prosperity. Many of the timber buildings in them were rebuilt in stone, and some, such as Catterick, Corbridge and Carlisle, became quite large towns with defences. The consequences for the environment must have been considerable. This was matched by the development of the colonia at York, which, under the reforms of the civil administration made by Severus, had become the capital of the new province of Britannia Inferior, whereas London remained the capital of the province of Britannia Superior.

There are also indications that in the north more cultivated land was under crops as opposed to pasture or rough grazing. The remnants of a Romano-British field system exist at Housesteads and others have been discovered associated with one of the few northern villas at Gargrave in Upper Airedale. Only seven examples of villas have been positively identified in Brigantia, and most of these cling to the strip of magnesian limestone which here flanks the eastern edge of the Pennines. The rock creates a very fertile soil and had been heavily settled in the Iron Age. Another area where extensive cultivation was being carried out was in the Cumbrian Plain south of Carlisle, although here the settlements were largely native in character, and the *pax Romana* had undoubtedly caused an increase in population.

The third century also saw another departure from the Roman strategy of keeping most of the British garrison in the north and in Wales. This was the introduction of coastal forts in the south and east, caused by the rise in piratical raiding. To begin with, forts were placed at Brancaster, at the mouth of the Wash, and at Reculver on the south side of the Thames estuary. They may have been joined by a naval base at Brough-on-Humber, although certainty has yet to be obtained. If it was a naval base, then the strategy of guarding the three main points of entry to the east coast, via the main river estuaries, was being implemented. The forts at Brancaster and Reculver were larger than normal, and could accommodate a naval detachment as well as the military garrison.

By the middle of the century the threat had greatly increased. This was first met by converting the triumphal monument at Richborough into a look-out post and surrounding it with earthworks. But before they were completed, plans were changed and work began on the construction of a massive masonry fort which, in another departure from earlier Roman military practice, had a very thick wall but no rampart behind it. Another fort was started at Burgh Castle in Suffolk, while others at Dover, Lympne (Kent), Bradwell (Essex) and Walton Castle (Suffolk) completed the chain for the time being. These forts were but part of a larger system, which covered both sides of the Channel.

In 286, Carausius, a commander of the British fleet, revolted against the central authority, retreated to Britain and was proclaimed emperor. He probably enlarged the system of coastal forts by building Portchester, near Chichester, and may have been responsible for extending it on the west coast with new estuarine forts at Cardiff, Caernarvon and Lancaster, although there is as yet no proof, and they may have belonged to a later period. The empire of Carausius was, however, short-lived. In 293 he was murdered by Allectus, his finance minister, whose reign was even shorter, for in 296 Constantius retook Britain for the western empire.

Britain now entered on another period of comparative prosperity. With the empire stabilized by the reforms of Diocletian, confidence returned and people were prepared to spend the reformed currency. Urban building was resumed, which may have partly been due to the release of masons by the completion of the long programme of fortifications. Certainly there were masons to spare because it is recorded that some were sent to help in the restoration of Autun (Gaul) after its destruction during a rebellion. But changes were incorporated in the towns of Britain, many of which are not fully understood. In some towns, such as Lincoln, buildings were now larger and better furnished, with greater space around them; mercantile enterprises seem to have been banished to the suburbs, although we cannot be certain of this. Many opulent domestic houses in the empire were often connected with trade, and some even had shops and workshops situated within them on the street frontages. That there was more space between houses is, however, in no doubt, and presumably, in the unlikely event that these spaces were left to nature, they were occupied by gardens and orchards. The overall effect must have been to make Lincoln much 'greener'. London is another curious case, which, it has been suggested, was in serious decline, with only some monumental buildings being constructed near the south-west corner. Yet London was now the capital of the newly created diocese as well as of the province of Maxima Caesariensis. It was walled by one of the longest circuits in Britain, and it is doubtful if this would have been envisaged if it was genuinely in a state of decline. Had it only been a case of protecting a group of administrative buildings at its centre, then surely a much shorter circuit of walls would have been built, as happened in some towns in Gaul. The central area including the forum and basilica at Wroxeter (fig. 45) had been destroyed by fire at the end of the third century and was not rebuilt. So the civitas had to make do without an administrative building. How they managed is not certain, but it suggests that there were changes also in the way these matters were handled. The site of the forum continued to be used and it may have provided an open-air market.

At Verulamium the theatre was rebuilt to a classical model, a new triumphal arch was erected outside it, and shops that had hitherto been of timber had been rebuilt in masonry. The forum and basilica at Cirencester were completely remodelled to provide accommodation for the governor, for the town had become the capital of one of the four provinces into which Britain was now divided. In other towns too, alterations and new buildings totally changed the urban scene.

But it was perhaps in the countryside that most changes took place. The first half of the fourth century was the zenith of the villa system. Although very large villas like Woodchester and Bignor emerged, it is still not possible to discern the ownership-tenant pattern. We can assume that they were the centres of large estates, and in some cases one can point to smaller villas whose land possibly lay within their compass, and where owners may have been tenants or managers. It is pointless to take the discussion further with our present knowledge. There was a tendency throughout most of the empire at this time for smaller estates and farms to be amalgamated into *latifundia*, which may have come about through the troubles of the third century, with small owners being bankrupted or dispossessed by other means. Another theory put forward is that there was a flight of capital from Gaul to Britain, caused by the barbarian invasions of the third century, which enabled refugees to buy up land and build villas on the Gallic scale, but there is no proof. The same period probably also saw the greatest extent of land under cultivation or pasture. Certainly one estate at Poxwell in Dorset extended its activities onto marginal land by construction of a lean-to building for industrial and agricultural processes, where iron ore was treated and cereals dried. But it did not last for long and by the middle of the fourth century the corn-driers had been dismantled and most of the masonry robbed.

Another development at this time was the emergence of a new type of villa, which would have had some impact on the countryside. They were based on aisled barns and in the simplest form would have consisted of a rectangular masonry or half-timbered building, with the internal space divided by two rows of pillars or timbers, which supported the roof, into a central nave and two aisles. Partitions separated the smaller part, as living quarters, from the rest, which presumably housed beasts and fodder. They are sometimes called basilican villas, and in certain instances such as at Stroud (Glos.) they formed the principal building and presumably accommodated both the farmer and his animals, not unlike the medieval long house; in some of the later examples they were expanded with rudimentary wings added and also modest bath-houses and even adorned with painted plaster. In one or two cases, massive foundations were used for one of the wings, far too great for normal domestic purpose, and it has been suggested that they formed the base of a tower granary. Consequently the effect on the landscape here implied would have been that much greater. In other cases as at Bignor (Sussex), these buildings were subsidiary to the main villa, or dwelling house, as part of a large complex of buildings, when they may have accommodated agricultural labourers, or simply served as barns, with fodder stored in the nave and beasts accommodated in the aisles.

Figure 45 Reconstruction drawing of Wroxeter, as seen from the north, sometime during the third century (reproduced by the kind permission of Ivan Lapper and English Heritage).

By the middle of the fourth century the prosperity of Britain and the villas in particular had peaked, and had already perhaps started to decline. The first signs of trouble came in 342, when the emperor Constans had to make an unplanned visit to the provinces in mid-winter. It is possible also that a detachment of the field army was then sent to Britain. This reflects the complete reorganization of the Roman army, which had taken place under Diocletian, into *limitanei*, who were static and served on the frontiers, and mobile units called *comitatenses*, who were expected to serve anywhere in a number of provinces as need arose. But in Britain the trouble under Constans was connected with a partial breakdown of Caracalla's earlier arrangements in the area beyond Hadrian's Wall, perhaps by a joint attack by the Picts from Scotland and Scots, who were still confined to northern Ireland. Moreover, Constans seemingly increased the forts of the Saxon Shore with the addition of Pevensey in the long gap between Lympne and Portchester. This was a fort unlike its predecessors in being shaped like an irregular oval, and would therefore have had a very different effect on the local land-scape; its construction suggests that there was increasing menace from Saxon raiders.

From then on there appear to have been a succession of invasions, which was not helped by the brief usurpation of Magnentius in 350. He probably took troops from the British garrison to Pannonia, where he was defeated at the battle of Mursa. Although he survived in Britain for two more years, his death brought extensive reprisals, as happened after the defeat of Clodius Albinus in the late second century, and may have started the decline of the land-owning class. Certainly occupation had ceased at a large number of villas before the end of that decade. However, it is not known if the abandonment of the domestic residence at the centre of an estate also led to the cessation of all agricultural activity. Much would have depended on matters for which we have no evidence, such as relationships between owners, managers, tenants and agricultural workers. It is likely, though, that if farming was continued it would have been on a reduced scale, with some of the land reverting to nature, beginning with the first growth of rank weeds and grass, followed by scrub and then larger trees. But one episode is worth recording to show that there had been no overall decline in agricultural productivity. Shortly after the Magnentian rebellion, the emperor Julian had a large fleet especially built to carry grain from Britain to the lower Rhine in order to relieve a famine. The historian Ammianus, who referred to this event, implied that the export of corn was a regular feature of British trade; presumably there was ample surplus for this trade.

Matters culminated in 367 with the barbarian conspiracy, when the Picts, Scots, Franks and Saxons acted in concert to attack Britain. A year later and Count Theodosius with four units of the field army was sent to restore order by the emperor Valentinian, who at that time was himself engaged against the Alamanni. The northern frontier was reorganized and where necessary rebuilt, possibly by groups of men from the southern civitates. But changes were incorporated and forts on the Wall became more like fortified towns, with women and children now accommodated within them. South of the Wall a number of forts were rebuilt to more normal standards and a chain of fortified signal stations was constructed on high ground on the Durham and Yorkshire coasts, north of Flamborough Head, to communicate with ships at sea, thus extending the efficacy of the Saxon Shore. Some work was put in hand in Wales and the naval base at Holyhead can probably be attributed to this period. Inland, towns seem to have escaped without damage, although it has been suggested that, in some cases, their defences were strengthened by the addition of external towers. Villas, as might be expected due to their more exposed positions, faired slightly less well, although at only a few can fire and destruction be attributed to enemy action. A group in Somerset and another in Hampshire, together with other isolated examples, such as Langton (Yorks.), seem to have suffered. But a large number were abandoned, probably owing to the general insecurity of the countryside, so hastening the actions which had begun in the 350s. However, those that survived, together with the towns on which they depended for their markets, continued to do well, and the reorganizations of Count Theodosius appear to have been effective.

These disturbances had some impact on industry, particularly the supply of pottery, which was now concentrated in the hands of fewer, large-scale producers. Thus those centres at Crambeck, Nene valley, Farnham, Thames valley and the New Forest greatly expanded their production at the expense of Hartshill, Isle of Purbeck and Colchester.

There was, however, another threat to the British coast, about which Count Theodosius could do nothing: a rise in sea level, which had begun probably about the beginning of the fourth century. By the middle of the century the harbour of the Saxon Shore fort at Lympne had silted badly, while the backing-up of inland rivers and springs, caused by the rise, led to serious landslips, which may have resulted in the destruction of the fort itself. It is possible that the construction of the new fort at Pevensey was intended to replace it. Two other sites were also affected. At Brough-on-Humber the harbour silted and in addition the walls at the south-west corner may have been breached. The fort at Portchester seems similarly to have been put out of commission and new construction at Bitterne on the river Itchen may have been designed to replace it. Results of this rise elsewhere, although indicated, have yet to be fully assessed.

The following years were punctuated by the rebellion of Magnus Maximus in 383. As before, when rebellion had occurred in Britain, he took a large part of the garrison to the Continent to support his claim; it is unlikely that they returned to Britain, although he probably did, and survived until 388 when he was executed by the emperor Theodosius. Following his death, the diocese of Britain came under the control of Valentinian II, emperor in the west. Now with a much reduced garrison it seems that the Picts, Saxons and Scots continued to raid the southern parts of the country with impunity until, in 396, the general Stilicho was sent to expel them, which was achieved three years later.

But by then, Italy was under threat from Alaric and the Visigoths; troops were required for its defence. Thus, although Stilicho could defeat the raiding parties which were threatening Britain, he could not strengthen the garrison. Indeed, it is more than likely that he removed yet further units.

By then also, the whole character of the Roman army had changed, with the increasing recruitment of barbarian tribes. These were normally organized into regiments of *milites* and *equites* – infantry and cavalry. The old legions had mostly been reduced in strength to a thousand men and had lost their superiority. So the next step was foreseeable. When Britain found itself unable to call upon enough regular troops, *foederati* were employed. These were normally Saxons or Franks, but may also have included Irish, who were given land (or subsidies) in exchange for military service. This recruitment may have begun as early as the beginning of the fifth century, or even before, although it was to reach its peak somewhat later.

The surviving regular army in Britain was left with a considerable burden, which it could not fulfil. Dissatisfied with their lot and with the actions of the central government, they rapidly proclaimed three emperors in quick succession. Two were rapidly disposed of, but the last, Constantine III, pleased them more. In the meantime affairs in Gaul had turned for the worse with a combined large-scale invasion of Vandals, Alans and Sueves, which was beginning to threaten the Channel coast. No other troops were available apart from those in Britain, and Constantine III immediately gathered what was left of the army and crossed to Gaul, where he successfully defeated the invaders and even regained control of Spain. But like his predecessors he was not content with his victory, and attempted to interfere in Italy, with the same ultimate fate: surrender to, and execution by, the emperor Honorius.

The people of Britain were angered by Constantine's actions, since it left the diocese virtually defenceless. So they threw out the remaining administrators of the central government; in 410 a letter arrived from Honorius addressed to the civitates in which he told them to organize their own defence. Thus ended official Roman intervention in Britain after 367 years.

For the next thirty to forty years the Britons seem to have been successful, with possibly the help of Saxon foederati, hoping perhaps that eventually the central government would reassert its authority. Certainly there are indications of bands of these people at Canterbury, Caister-by-Norwich and Dorchester-on-Thames. It was a time when strong men came into their own and one such was Vortigern, whose name means 'high king'; another was Ambrosius. Neither was all contact with Rome lost; it was maintained through the Church, and St Germanus, bishop of Auxerre, was sent to combat the Pelagian heresy which was dividing the country.

Vortigern seems to have been the first-recorded leader officially to have settled Saxon federates in Kent and possibly other parts of the country. Eventually they rebelled against him, and the ruling classes appealed to Rome once more – the Groans of the Britons – but this time it went unanswered, and the Saxons seem to have taken over much of eastern England. Yet something of the old order still survived in the west, Wales and the north-west even beyond the gradual creep of Saxon dominance in the sixth and seventh centuries.

What of the countryside in this disturbed period? As has been shown already, the towns and villas enjoyed a period of prosperity in the late fourth century, even though there were fewer of the latter. There is nothing to suggest that much of this prosperity did not continue into the early fifth. Commerce and trade, which were the staple of their existence, must have continued unabated, and with them presumably the cultivation of land. But gradual changes can be seen. A corn-drier inserted into the room of a house at Verulamium suggests that crops had to be carried quickly within the walls for safety; one of the Saxon's main methods of warfare was to burn standing crops. The forum at Cirencester was still being cleaned after 430, even though the paving stones had worn out. The baths basilica at Wroxeter had been converted into a succession of timber-framed buildings (fig. 46), while the tombstone of a man of Irish descent implies the possible presence of federates. An Ogham stone at Silchester and the enclosing of the area round the town by large dykes suggests the likelihood of more Irish federates and the maintenance of a non-Saxon enclave.

Most of the villas which had survived so far do not appear to have suffered much damage; there are signs of destruction at North Wraxall (Wilts.) and Lullingstone

Figure 46 Reconstruction drawing of fifth-century timber-framed houses in the ruins of the baths basilica at Wroxeter (reproduced by the kind permission of Ivan Lapper and English Heritage).

Figure 47 Early regeneration of natural chalkland; there is a growth of long, coarse grass first, which smothers more delicate downland plants. Later, small bushes such as hawthorn or blackthorn seed themselves; in this picture they are just beginning to take over.

(Kent), but the rest slid into decay with declining standards of living, until the collapse of markets and the breakdown in transport caused their ultimate abandonment. However, it was very much an individual abandonment; what affected one may not have affected the villa next door, and there are isolated examples, such as Great Casterton (Rutland) and Langton (Yorks.), where a measure of prosperity is known to have survived into the fifth century. But it is interesting that Gildas writing in the middle of the sixth century does not mention villas, implying that by then not even a tradition was left.

The same was probably true of industry. Deprived of their markets, the pottery, iron and other centres of manufacturing processes could not survive except on a very local basis. Thus the flourishing potteries of the late fourth century hardly lasted into the fifth, despite their massive production. The ironworks of the Weald and Forest of Dean were isolated from major towns, and no longer was there any great demand for lead, although lead pipes were still being used to carry water at Verulamium. Likewise, with no masonry buildings being constructed, quarries were closed and abandoned; there was ample stone to be plundered from ruins, if it was needed. Roads and streets were left in disrepair, illustrated by the rutted state of the road in its final stages leading west from Cirencester.

So ultimately the countryside returned to what it had been before the arrival of the Romans, and even before the later Iron Age. Small pockets of survivors, together with the new Saxon villages, would have continued to cultivate small parcels of land, returning largely to a subsistence agriculture. Land left uncultivated would, in the absence of the rabbit, soon have reverted to nature with the regeneration first of coarse

Figure 48 Final regeneration of natural chalkland. Fifty years ago this wooded area was a grassy bank with turf close-cropped by rabbits. The arrival of myxomatosis allowed the trees to grow unchecked.

grass, then of scrub (fig. 47), then of woods and forests (fig. 48), which can occur in as little as fifty years; without intensive grazing, heather moorland would have been revitalized; drains and ditches would have become blocked, leading to the reforming of marshland. Gradually Roman masonry buildings would collapse, eventually to become grassy mounds covering the ruins; only in towns would portions sometimes survive, being incorporated into later buildings, like the Jewry Wall at Leicester, or the Old Work at Wroxeter. Defences provided lines for new town walls. Roads would become green lanes, if they survived at all, often to be the boundaries of future parishes. So began the process from which the English landscape was created, much of it being inherited from Roman Britain.

9

ROMAN SURVIVAL IN
THE MODERN LANDSCAPE

It is surprising how much modern Britain has inherited from the Romans, and how many traces of their presence are still to be seen in the landscape. These range from standing monuments, to grass-covered mounds in fields, to sites which are only visible, under certain conditions, from the air. Moreover, we have to remember that the Romans' choice of a site, whether for a fort, town or villa, very much depended on the ideal geographical position within a given area, with, in the case of military sites, contemporary tactical or strategical considerations which rarely exist today. Consequently we find many medieval and modern towns and villages situated on top of their Roman predecessors mainly by accident of geography, not through continuity of settlement. Some did move, though, to take advantage of slightly more ideal conditions in the middles ages; thus Silchester became Reading, Wroxeter moved to Shrewsbury and Verulamium to St Albans. Even then a small village nucleus often remained behind. Villas equally were sometimes the source for the growth of villages and monastic communities for the same geographical reasons and not from any sense of continuity. It has been suggested, for instance, that the seventh-century monastic estate at Withington (Glos.) may reflect that of the earlier villa, and there are many other cases where a villa preceded a village, often with the church sitting on or near the ruins. It could be that these same ruins provided a close and convenient quarry for building stone.

The three permanent legionary fortresses constructed in Britain still have upstanding remains. York, where much of the walls survive, especially part of the noted river front with its multangular external towers, is a good example. Here, Roman strategic siting was followed in subsequent periods. For much of the middle ages, and even more recently, it was the military centre for the north of England. Now, in addition to the walls, one can see part of the principia, excavated below the Minster. Chester, likewise, was in a good strategic position, separating the north of England from Wales. Here, lengths of the walls also stand, and in addition part of the amphitheatre has been excavated and displayed, while the Roman harbour wall – the Roodee Wall – is visible on the race-course. Both Chester and York have given rise to flourishing modern towns.

Caerleon, although tactically and strategically placed in the early Roman period, was already beginning to decline in importance during the third and fourth centuries, in favour of coastal sites, such as Cardiff. It retained some tactical advantages in the early middle ages, when a motte-and-bailey castle was built near the eastern angle of the fortress. Parts of the west walls can now be seen, together with the amphitheatre and legionary bath-house, which have been excavated and displayed. Barrack blocks have also been exposed near the western corner in Prysg Field. Most of the line of the buried wall can be traced in modern streets and property boundaries.

Of the earlier fortresses, nothing is visible above the surface except at Inchtuthil, where the outline of the wall and ditches appear as grass-covered undulations in very flat fields. It is almost the only legionary fortress in the empire which is completely unencumbered by later buildings.

Numerous examples of other military installations survive in Britain, either as grass-covered mounds or as standing masonry. Most campaign camps are known only from aerial photography, but at a number in Wales, the north of England and Scotland, such as Y Pygwn (Dyfed), Malam (Yorks.), Rey Cross (Cumbria) and Pennymuir (Borders), the line of the ramparts or ditches can still be traced on the surface. Similarly, the practice siege-works below the hillfort at Burnswark (Dumfries) still stand out remarkably vividly, with the three ballista platforms facing up the hill.

Auxiliary forts of the invasion period are again mostly known from aerial photographs, such as Great Casterton (Rutland), or else they are buried deep beneath Roman towns as at Cirencester. But the fort tucked into the north-west corner of the Iron Age hillfort at Hod Hill (Dorset) is still visible and displays the widely set ditches which were characteristic of the Claudio-Neronian period. An unusual timber fort of the Neronian period has been excavated and partly reconstructed at the Lunt, near Coventry. The east defences followed a sinuous course and a length has been rebuilt, together with the timber-framed east gate (fig. 49). A granary (fig. 50) has also been reconstructed together with the gyrus. The latter was a circular open space bounded by a timber stockade and with a single funnelled entrance, which may have been used as a cavalry training ground. Other buildings have been marked out on the ground with concrete.

Masonry forts tend to leave more visible evidence of their presence, but are chiefly confined to Wales, the north of England and Scotland; many were multi-period, so it is normally only the latest period which shows on the surface. They can range in size from about 1 ha, which could house a quingenary cohort of infantry, up to nearly 4 ha for a milliary cavalry unit. In Wales and the hinterland of the northern frontiers they tended to lie a day's march apart, a distance of 20–30 km; on the frontiers they were more closely spaced.

Two of the finest examples of auxiliary forts to be seen anywhere in the Roman Empire are at Whitley Castle (Northumberland) and Ardoch (Perthshire). Both are multi-period sites, which can be best appreciated at the latter. Another fort in Northumberland is at Risingham, which was one of the outpost forts of Hadrian's Wall, and which was occupied almost to the end of the Roman period. Here can be seen not only the clear outline of the defences, but also a series of low banks in the interior, covering possibly the latest buildings, or perhaps a post-Roman settlement. Yet another fort in Cumbria, near the southern end of the Lake District, is Hardknott, noted for its impressive position guarding the road that runs over Hardknott Pass. The defences and some of the internal buildings have been cleared and also a small external bath-house. The chief interest, though, is the parade ground, levelled out of the hillside, some 230 m outside the east gate; although all forts would have had them, this is one of the few in Britain where it is still visible.

In Wales two of the best survivals among auxiliary forts are at Brecon and Caernarvon. At the former, the outline of the defences can easily be traced, while three of the gates

Figure 49 Restored eastern gate at the Lunt, near Coventry.

have been completely excavated and cleared. At Caernarvon, part of the defences can be seen. Most of the other forts are only visible from the air, but sometimes in very dry summers it is possible to make out on the ground the parch marks of internal streets and buildings, as at Castell Collen and Forden Gaer.

It is difficult to select sites from the two northern frontiers, which are best preserved in both central sections. Although both frontier lines are reasonably well marked, their political failings are demonstrated by the fact that neither became the ultimate frontier between England and Scotland. The Antonine Wall was too far north while Hadrian's Wall was too far south. This is true of most of the frontiers of the Roman Empire; only on the lower Danube, once Dacia had been abandoned, is there correspondence with the modern frontier along the river between Romania and Bulgaria.

Hadrian's Wall itself is probably best seen in the length at Walltown, where the narrow wall stands to some considerable height, and the method of construction can

Figure 50 Restored granary at the Lunt, near Coventry.

be appreciated. The stones forming the faces are laid horizontally, and not in line with the slope of the hill. Other good sections survive either side of the forts at Birdoswald and Housesteads. The former fort is situated in a singular position with the rear overlooking the steep escarpment of the river Irthing. The line of its defences can clearly be seen, as well as two of its gates. The fort at Housesteads also has much of its interior displayed, as well as the vicus, and possesses a good site museum. The fort at Chesters also has a museum and is one of the most accessible; parts of the defences are exposed as well as some of the internal buildings. To be seen nearby are the well-preserved bath-house and the east abutment of the bridge which carried the Wall over the river North Tyne; a mill-leet runs through its middle. The abutment of another bridge can be seen at Willowford at the crossing of the river Irthing.

Immediately to the rear of the Wall lies the military road and the vallum. Both can be observed in a good state of preservation east of Haltwhistle Burn, where the relationship between them can also be appreciated, the military way clearly being later. On the Wall above them is Cawfields Milecastle (Milecastle 42). The most interesting part of the ditch in front of the Wall is at Limestone Corner, where great blocks of stone lie where the Romans left them, as being too difficult to split and remove; some contain the impressions of Roman tool marks.

South of the vallum lie a number of forts, which were part of the first planning of the frontier. Such a one is Chesterholm, where excavations have been carried out over recent years, and much is now to be seen especially in the vicus; it lies some 3 km south-west of Housesteads. Corbridge lies further east near the point where Dere Street crossed the Wall. There was a succession of forts here which were ultimately replaced in the early third century by two new military works compounds, a pair of large granaries and an uncompleted large square building with a central courtyard, which may have been intended to be a macellum; these have been excavated and left exposed to view. A town grew around them, which is known largely from aerial photographs, although traces of the defences can be seen as earth mounds near the north-west and north-east corners.

The Antonine Wall, and most of its forts, being built of turf and timber, left very different traces from those of Hadrian's Wall. One of the best surviving sections runs from Watling Lodge, near Falkirk, to just east of Bonnybridge, and contains the fort at Rough Castle. The ditch is particularly clear. There is an unusual feature at Rough Castle, which is rare in Roman fortifications. Just beyond the Wall, outside the fort, is an area of *lilia*. These were pits dug in a quincunx formation so that one row overlapped the spaces in the row before, and so on. When covered with foliage and rough grass, they would provide a trap for the unwary attacker. Another section which survives well lies on the high ground of the central part, where the forts of Croy Hill and Bar Hill were situated. Two unusual features can be followed near Croy Hill, where the ditch was not dug owing to the hardness of the rock (fig. 15), and where it diverges outwards from the line of the Wall rampart to skirt the hill at a lower level. Bar Hill is the only fort which is completely detached from the back face of the Wall.

Minor works of the army can be seen at a number of places. Most important were the signal stations, usually a tower built of timber which was surrounded by a turf or earth rampart and a ditch. Some were members of a series, such as those on the Gask Ridge (Perthshire) and the Stainmore Pass across the Pennines. Other single ones were placed to afford an enhanced view. Thus that at the southern entrance to the Sma' Glen near the fort at Fendoch had a view, not only up the glen, which was hidden from the fort, but also of the fort itself; it could therefore signal an advance warning of an attack (figs 13 and 14). In the later Roman period, these signal towers were built of stone and surrounded by a masonry wall. Once there was a chain of them on the Yorkshire coast, but the only surviving remains are to be seen near the cliff edge in the grounds of Scarborough Castle.

Practice camps are another manifestation of the army. They were small earthworks, seldom enclosing more than 20–30 m sq., which display all the characteristics of full-sized turf and timber fort defences: turf rampart, ditch, *claviculae* and/or *titula*. Doubtless constructed as field exercises, they were intended to familiarize recruits in the use of turf as a building material; some skill is needed to handle cut turves, especially on rounded corners. They usually occur in groups and the best example in Britain is at Llandrindod Common (Powys) where a group of eighteen is situated some 2–3 km from the parent fort. Others are to be seen near Tomen-y-Mur and Gelligaer Common in Wales, and one north of the legionary fortress at York; these have now been destroyed.

But probably the finest survivals among the works of the Roman army are the late Saxon Shore forts on the south-eastern coast. Some, it is true, have disappeared from view; Dover for instance lies beneath the modern town, while Walton Castle was destroyed by coastal erosion. Even its site is now in dispute. But the massive walls still stand at Burgh Castle, Reculver, Richborough, Lympne, Pevensey and Portchester. At Richborough also can be seen the deep foundations of the triumphal monument. Lympne has been reduced to a jumbled mass of masonry, due to land slip, while

Brancaster, where no walls survive above the surface, can still be traced on the ground by the course of its ditch.

Most of the towns, both large and some small, of Roman Britain became perpetuated in the medieval and modern periods. Little of these is to be seen standing above the surface, as much of the Roman material lies deeply buried, sometimes by as much as 3–5 m beneath the modern surface, except perhaps where the modern version of the town is smaller than its Roman counterpart. Then sometimes the line of the defences can been followed, either as an earth bank, or as a road or as a line in modern property boundaries. Such is the case at Cirencester, Towcester and Ilchester. In some cases the line of the defences was followed by the medieval walls, as at Canterbury, Gloucester and partly at York. Otherwise, little or nothing survives, as at Leicester or London, although at London short lengths of the walls are still standing at the Tower of London and at London Wall. But in nearly all cases the confines of the Roman towns defined those of the middle ages, and even put a constraint on modern property boundaries; thus the Romans left a lasting imprint on the landscape, even though it is not now visible as Roman.

The towns which still show best were those where migration occurred in the post-Roman period to nearby sites, leaving the Roman ones to become open fields, with perhaps the nucleus of a small village. Wroxeter moved to Shrewsbury, Verulamium to St Albans, Silchester to Reading, Caerwent to Chepstow and Caistor-by-Norwich to Norwich; each though retained a small village or hamlet, although at the last site there is little more than a church. Among the 'small' towns, complete abandonment was more often the norm, and no modern buildings clutter the sites of Dorn, Kenchester, Chesterton-on-Fosse, Thorpe-by-Newark or Water Newton; only farms exist at Catterick and Irchester.

The lengths of surviving wall at London have already been mentioned. Much of the alignment of the south wall is retained by Upper and Lower Thames Streets. Something of the street grid, especially near the gates, is preserved in the lines of Aldgate, Bishopsgate, Cheapside and Ludgate Hill, but most of the remainder has disappeared. Nevertheless one of the axes of the associated fort has remained as Cripplegate. Modern London Bridge has moved slightly upstream, so the southern approach has been relocated.

London is by no means the best example to demonstrate the survival of streets in post-Roman contexts. Usually the lines of at least the two main axes reappear in the medieval and modern towns, but not here. At Colchester, for instance, the main east–west street of the Roman town reappears, in modified form, as the High Street, although it is reduced at its west end to little more than a dead-end lane and a foot passage passing through the Balkerne Gate. The street which connected the North Gate with Headgate survives as North Hill. Lincoln is slightly less fortunate; Bailgate marks the line of the main north–south street of the upper town, but the east–west line is interrupted by the castle at its west end. In the southern part of the city there is little correspondence and only High Street, emerging through the south gate, or in later times the Stonebow, follows the same line as its Roman predecessor. The wall from the Newport Arch (the North Gate of the Upper Town which still partly stands) can be followed for a length eastwards and contains, attached to its rear face, the water tank of the *castellum divisiorum*, from which water from the aqueduct was distributed to the nearby bath-house and through the town. Another gate, the west gate of the lower town, has been excavated and is displayed near the city council offices. The Mint Wall is also worthy of notice, since it probably represents the rear wall of the basilica; it still stands to a height of 7.25 m, and runs for a distance of 22.5 m. Put-log holes occur at frequent intervals.

At Gloucester, one of the main axes survives as Northgate Street and Southgate Street, where the latter, however, crosses the forum site to join the former. Eastgate Street starts as true to line, but Westgate Street, which joins it, diverts slightly to the north of the old line. The street plan of Canterbury in the medieval period became warped and only Castle Street closely follows the line of its Roman predecessor to the Worth Gate. St Peter's Street coincides near the Westgate; the remainder of that axis diverges from the Roman line to exit at St George's Gate, which had no earlier counterpart. Much of the circuit of the walls was reused in the middle ages, and varying amounts of Roman work survive within its core. The most impressive section survives where it was incorporated into the north wall of the church of St Mary Northgate; it stands in a much patched form, with possible crenellations at the top, to a height of 5 m (fig. 51).

Canterbury also exhibits two more unusual features. When excavations were being undertaken in Burgate in 1945, it was found that a late second-century wall actually formed the boundary between two medieval, and hence pre-1942, properties. The wall rose to within about 0.6 m of the surface and one face, which had been cut back, acted as the cellar wall. The other feature was in the St George's Street bath-house, where it was found that one cellar of a more modern building had been cut down to the upper floor of a hypocaust, which had been reused as the cellar floor; constant shovelling of coal on this surface had worn some holes in it, through which coal had fallen into the hypocaust beneath. Remarkable instances of continuity!

Nothing survives at Chelmsford except the line of the main north–south street axis. At Verulamium, now only marked by the village of St Michael's, parts of the town wall can still be seen, especially at the southern end, including the remains of internal and external towers near the south corner. The outline of the London gate has been laid out. The ditches are also particularly fine in the same section. Internally, the theatre has been excavated and displayed, while next door to it are the outlines of shops in Insula XIV. Another house with mosaics, in the centre of Insula IV, can also be seen in part. There is an excellent museum.

At Wroxeter, where doubt has been, wrongly, cast on the existence of a wall, the defences only show as a low, widely spread, earth mound on the north east and south sides; on the west side, however, the river has encroached. But the bath-house, together with the Old Work, a wall which divided the bath's basilica from the baths proper, has been excavated and can still be seen together with the adjacent market hall; also displayed is the eastern portico of the forum. The defences at Leicester have been completely obscured by modern buildings, although their line has been roughly preserved in the modern street plan, as has the north–south axis. Another of the finest pieces of standing Roman masonry in Britain survives in the Jewry Wall, which, like the Old Work at Wroxeter, separated the main bath-house from the palaestra; it probably still stands because at one stage it was incorporated in nearby St Nicholas Church. Part of the bath-house, although covered by the museum, can still be seen, especially some very fine drains. Outside the town, a short length of the aqueduct has been preserved at the Raw Dykes on Aylestone Road.

Figure 51 The north wall of St Mary Northgate, Canterbury, which contains elements of the Roman town wall standing to a height of 5 m.

Caistor-by-Norwich is another town which migrated, leaving the old site with only a church near its south-east corner. Although the wall is not visible, its line is well-marked by a high bank. Nothing is to be seen in the interior, but in very hot, dry weather the streets stand out as parch marks.

A small group of towns exhibit much the same features: Chichester, Winchester, Exeter, Dorchester and Cirencester. The lines of the main street axes survive in the modern streets, but with occasional warping, and the lines of the defences are more or less preserved by modern streets or property boundaries, or sometimes by short lengths of surviving masonry. Dorchester is interesting because of the partial preservation of the aqueduct line west of the town where it skirts the Iron Age hillfort at Poundbury and thence by a sinuous course along the contours as far as Frampton, where the source lay in a small stream. At Cirencester, the road from the Verulamium to the Bath Gates is perpetuated by London Road, Lewis Lane and Querns Road, but the north–south axis has become mostly obscured, with only the north end marked by Dollar Street. The defences are best seen near the north-east and south-east corners where they appear as a bank of varying height; a length, together with internal and external towers, has been exposed just north of the Verulamium Gate. The amphitheatre, now cleared of its trees and scrub, lies as grass-covered mounds marking the seating banks, outside the Bath Gate.

One of the finest surviving examples of town walls in Britain is at Caerwent. The town itself is now occupied by a large village, but the walls were never incorporated in medieval defences. Thus on the whole of the south side and parts of the north side Roman work still stands almost to the height of the wall walk. There are also six external towers of polygonal form on the south with three more surviving on the north side, together with the north and south gates. The main street of the modern village follows the line of the east–west axis, with parts of the equivalent gates at either end. A row of shops near the forum has been excavated and displayed.

The last major town to consider is Aldborough. Here again a large village occupies the site, although the small town of Boroughbridge nearby suggests that some migration took place. The line of the defences can be followed along most of their course and small parts have been displayed on the south side. The east–west axis is followed in a rather warped form by one of the main streets of the village, but only the southern part of the north–south axis is represented by a modern counterpart. There is a small site museum.

Continuity among the 'small towns' is more varied; many gave rise to modern villages, but only a few blossomed into towns. Quite a number remain as open fields with nothing to see above the surface. Since there were over fifty of these towns, it is not possible to deal with them individually, so they will be grouped according to how they survived and consequently to the effects they still have on the urban and rural landscapes.

'Small towns' with sizeable towns over them include Carlisle, Rochester, Bath, Alcester, Cambridge, Godmanchester, Buxton and Towcester among others. There is little to see at Carlisle although the line of the putative wall can be followed for part of its course. Much the same is true of many of these sites, with Roman features almost entirely obscured. At Bath, major parts of the Great Baths have been displayed, while the line of the wall is marked along half of its length by modern streets; nothing is known of the Roman street plan, either here or at Carlisle. Watling Street still keeps roughly to its old course through Towcester and Rochester. At the former site the banks covering the walls are still visible on the east side and near the north-west corner; likewise at Rochester the line of the wall, especially on the east side, can be made out in modern features. Although Buxton was a Roman spa, similar to Bath, no trace now exists in the modern town.

A number of 'small towns' are today marked by villages of variable size. Good examples are Ancaster, where Ermine Street bisects it into two unequal halves and the line of the defences can be followed with ease; Great Casterton, similarly bisected by Ermine Street and where the line of the fourth-century ditch is particularly clear on the east side; and Dorchester-on-Thames, where the defences can be followed on the west side. Sometimes, as in the case of Mancetter, the village has migrated a short distance away leaving the Roman site largely free of modern buildings; the defences are indicated by hedge lines, with the northern part marked by the late ditch; Watling Street cuts through the middle. Catterick is a similar example, although here the modern village moved much further south; there is little to see of the Roman town, although extensive excavations were carried out before the construction of the by-pass, which cuts through the site in a deep cutting.

Many of the sites are now completely open fields, sometimes with a farm situated in one corner. The lines of internal streets can often be seen in very hot, dry weather, and occasionally one of the main roads runs on a slight agger. The defences usually act as modern field boundaries and are often marked by hedges or rows of trees. Water Newton is an excellent example lying astride the Roman line of Ermine Street, but Irchester, Mildenhall, Alchester, Kenchester and Chesterton-on-Fosse are all equally good, again with the lines of the defences picked out in hedgerows. The last site has the Fosse Way running through the middle, its modern line closely conforming to the earlier line; on the west side the defences are clearly marked by the bank and ditch.

Rome placed its stamp on Britain most effectively in its road system, which even now controls much of the country. 'The course of the roads was evidently planned with skill, and laid out with a complete grasp of the general features of a country to be passed through.' Thus wrote Codrington in 1903 in his book *Roman Roads in Britain*. This can be demonstrated by taking only two examples, already mentioned in a preceding chapter. Watling Street is aimed in the general direction of Watford Gap, the lowest point in the hills traversing the Midlands. Likewise the Fosse Way never deviates more than 10 km either side of its two terminal points at Lincoln and Seaton in Devon; clearly a knowledge of the overall routes was familiar to the Roman surveyors.

Before the construction of by-passes in the 1930s and the motorway network, which began in the 1950s and is still continuing, most of the main trunk roads in England, Scotland and Wales owed their origin to Roman surveyors and engineers. There were divergences created in medieval and more modern times, it is true, but main alignments still held good. Diversions occurred presumably when lengths became impassable for one reason or another. One of the most remarkable survivals is the line of the Fosse Way, since, between Leicester and Cirencester, it avoids all modern towns. It takes, but never directly coincides with, the line of the prehistoric trackway known as the Jurassic Way, which kept to the high ground along the Jurassic ridge. The ancient line is lost to the modern road system just south of Leicester for a distance of some kilometres in the region of High Cross, but it soon picks up the old line again, and after a considerable length as country lanes, it rejoins the major, modern road system at Halford. Indeed, recent improvements to the lanes have produced a very convenient direct route from the north-east Midlands to the south-west. In places it still runs on the old agger. Even where the modern road network diverges from it, the line is often marked by a track, a footpath, a grass-covered bank, a parish or a property boundary.

Most of the modern main roads radiating from London owe their origins to the Romans and have thus indelibly imprinted themselves on the landscape. Some are lost in the suburbs, but not all; Edgeware Road, leading north from Marble Arch, follows the line of Watling Street, as does the section nearer the City following Ludgate Hill, Fleet Street and much of the Strand. One of the best examples of Roman road construction is Stane Street, which begins at London Bridge on a course which points directly to the east gate of Chichester. Thereafter it diverges from the main alignment from point to point to follow the easiest route over the intervening high land of the North Downs, the Weald and the South Downs, before taking a secondary alignment at the top of the last high point on the South Downs towards Chichester.

Away from London, survival is sometimes just as good. Dere Street, the main road north from York, follows the line of the old Great North Road as far as Scotch Corner, where it diverges onto a minor road via Piercebridge to Corbridge and beyond. Another road branches westwards at Scotch Corner and its line is followed by the modern road, through the Stainmore Pass, on to Carlisle. A good example of the competence of Roman surveying is to be seen in Shropshire, in the west Midlands, where the road from Wroxeter to Kenchester, preserved as a continuous hedge line, aims for and curves through the Church Stretton gap, leaving the hills to either side.

Similarly, the road through the Lune Gorge in Cumbria, again marked by an almost continuous hedge line, is the best approach to Carlisle, between the hills of the Lake District and the Pennines. The same course is used today by both the M6 motorway and the London–Glasgow railway line.

These last two examples show how a Roman road, even if it is still not in use, can leave its mark on the landscape by way of field, property and often parish boundaries.

The reason behind the survival, in one form or another, of the main roads of the Roman system lies probably in their construction. They were usually raised on an agger or an embankment bounded by ditches for drainage, and were formed from several layers of aggregate, rammed hard to make a good running surface. Consequently, even if not used as a road today, the banks made very convenient, visible lines on which to lay out boundaries. Lesser tracks did not receive such treatment. In the first place they were not surveyed in a series of straight sections; there was probably no agger and they may have been left unmetalled. Quite often they became hollow-ways. A well-used track at Empingham, near Rutland Water, which seems to have been associated with a nearby villa, consisted of a slight hollow-way, a central depression caused by the passage of draft animals, and a pair of ruts made by the wheels of carts. Consequently, there is little to survive in the landscape; most rapidly grassed over, once traffic had ceased, leaving nothing to show on the surface, except perhaps a slight depression, and often they can now only be detected with the aid of aerial photography. Many droveways have been found by this method in the Fens and on the South Downs, meandering through the countryside.

The Roman country landscape survived less well. Often by accident of geography a villa site is marked by a modern village, but it only goes to show how well the site was chosen in the first place. The most prominent features which now appear in the landscape, although in sadly reduced numbers, are the various field systems (fig. 52). At one time their lynchets used to cover much of the chalk country of the South Downs, the Marlborough Downs, Salisbury Plain and Dorset, but modern agriculture has removed most of them. Only in a few, carefully preserved places can they now be seen. Most are of the so-called Celtic variety, which usually continued without change in the Roman period. At Martin Down, in Hampshire, a good block has survived, where can also be seen Roman attempts to convert some of the Celtic fields into the more-developed 'long' fields. Similar observations can be made at Fyfield Down (Wilts.) and Smacam Down (Dorset). Once many hectares of ancient fields existed in the Fens, where they were outlined by the ditches which served as their boundaries in these flat lands. Only few have been left by the onward march of modern agriculture; most, including lengths of the Car Dyke, are now only visible from the air. The Car Dyke, part of a Roman drainage system, ran along the Fen edge from the river Ouse, near Peterborough, to the river Witham in Lincolnshire, and was used to impound the water flowing off the higher land to the west, until it could be released to the sea on the ebb tide. Further north, in the Pennines, over a hundred hectares of ancient fields can be seen at Grassington in Upper Wharfdale.

Villas seldom show any traces in the landscape. But several have been excavated and left exposed to view. Chedworth (Glos.) and Lullingstone (Kent) are the prime examples. Much can also be seen of Great Witcombe (Glos.), while that at Littlecote Park (Wilts.) has been exposed, but with some reconstruction. Likewise at Bignor (Sussex), a good deal of the main house has been laid out. At Fishbourne (Sussex), if it can be included among

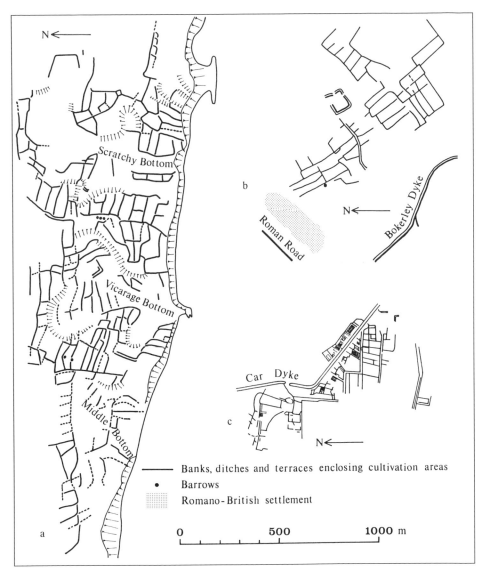

Figure 52 Field systems at (a) Chaldon Herring (Dorset); (b) Martin Down (Hants). In both some squarish 'Celtic' fields have been converted to longer fields by the removal of lynchets, so as to accommodate heavier ploughs (both after the Royal Commission on Historical Monuments for England); (c) Cottenham (Cambs.) showing groups of small plots (after P. Salway).

villas, parts of the main wings of the palace have been left open, as also at Brading in the Isle of Wight. The 'villa' on the cliffs at Folkestone was once visible, but deterioration was so bad that it was decided to rebury it; it has been disputed as to whether it was a true villa or the residence of an officer of the Saxon Shore.

Most unexcavated sites can therefore be seen best from the air, but there are one or two exceptions. Before excavations started, the villa at Barnsley, near Cirencester, showed as a rectangular platform, while some of the field walls survived as grass-covered mounds in pasture that had never been ploughed since the Roman period. At Beadlam in north Yorkshire, again before excavation, some of the villa walls could be seen, covered by turf, standing above general ground level.

Native villages are better represented, more especially in highland areas where there has been less subsequent interference in the countryside, such as the north, Wales and the south-west. An exception in the south is Chisenbury Warren, lying on the north-east side of Salisbury Plain. The site covers nearly 6 ha and is surrounded by a large area of Celtic fields. A wide street meanders through the centre on either side of which are about eighty rectangular hollows, presumably representing the remains of buildings. But in the north, many more native settlements occur as turf-covered banks or the debris of drystone walls. One of the best examples is Ewe Close (Cumbria), which lies beside the main Roman road leading north to Carlisle, where an extensive farm grew up containing circular buildings and sub-rectangular and rectangular enclosures. In the south-west, the characteristic survival is the village of courtyard houses, of which the partly exposed site at Chysauster, near Penzance, is best presented; many rounds can also be seen, such as that on Tregonning Hill. In Wales, regional differences can be detected, from the ring-works in the south-west, such as Cwmbrwyn, to the late Roman reuse of an Iron Age hillfort at Dinorben in the north-east.

Religious sites fair equally badly as villas in the survival pattern. There are, of course, the baths at Bath, already mentioned above, which were part of the great religious establishment centred round the temple of Sulis Minerva. But the temple itself lies beneath the modern pump room, and although parts were revealed in the basement, nothing can be seen. The foundations of the Temple of Claudius at Colchester have also been mentioned. There, the earth-filled masonry vaults which formed the podium have been emptied and can be visited under the castle. A row of classically inspired temples at Corbridge has been excavated and the foundations left exposed, while the temple of Mithras in London was bodily removed from the site and reconstructed nearby. It lay for many years mouldering away in a basement as an example of misplaced public opinion. Fortunately the Mithraeum at Carrawburgh, on Hadrian's Wall, has been excavated and can still be seen, together with reproductions of the altars and statuary which were found inside it. At Richborough, in the north-west corner of the Saxon Shore fort, lies one of the few visible traces of Christianity. It is a brick-built, hexagonal font, which belonged to a timber-built church, lying to its south; it dates probably to the late fourth or early fifth century. The villa at Lullingstone was also associated with Christianity, but although now on view, the domestic chapel was on an upper floor above the basement room, into which it had collapsed.

The only funerary monuments which show above the surface are barrows. Roman barrows were restricted to the south-east; sometimes they line main roads, while others have been recorded near villas. One of the best groups is the Bartlow Hills (Essex) where four large burial mounds survive out of a group of eight, and may have been associated with a nearby villa.

There is still much to see of Roman Britain above the surface. Even more lies largely unnoticed underground, but continues to exert its effect on modern topography to an extent which many people do not realize. Rome, in 367 years of occupation, left a permanent mark on the British landscape that will not be easily wiped away.

FURTHER READING

As far as possible this section is confined to matters dealt with in the text. General aspects of Roman Britain can be obtained from any number of sources, of which there are more than enough.

First and foremost for any understanding of the subject are the two sheets of the 1:625,000 *Geological Survey of Great Britain* (BGS, 1992) to which might be added D.G.A. Whitten and J.R.V. Brooks, *The Penguin Dictionary of Geology* (Harmondsworth, 1981); still useful is C. Fox, *The Personality of Britain* (Cardiff, 1932) even though it was published many years ago. There is no modern, comprehensive survey of the climate of the British Isles, so again we must fall back on B.G. Bilham, *The Climate of the British Isles* (London, 1938). For vegetation P.J.N. Havins, *The Forests of England* (Newton Abbot, 1976) is useful, as is also P. Beswick and I.D. Rotherham (eds), *Ancient Woodlands: Their Archaeology and Ecology* (Sheffield, 1993) together with a very recent publication G. Roberts, *Woodlands of Kent: Timber Trees, Coppice and Country Park* (Ashford, 1999). The monumental work by R. Mabey, *Flora Britannica* (London, 1996) is not a systematic botanical book, but rather a combined botanical, historical and mythological compendium on British plants of all species. Another, more botanical, book of British wild flowers is W. Keble Martin, *The Concise British Flora in Colour* (London, 1969). Man's appearance in the landscape is covered by two volumes of collected papers, J.G. Evans, S. Limbrey and H. Cleere (eds), *The Effect of Man on the Landscape: the Highland Zone* (London, 1975) and S. Limbrey and J.G. Evans (eds), *The Effect of Man on the Landscape: the Lowland Zone* (London, 1978). The effects of rising and falling sea level are considered in a series of collected papers, F.H. Thompson (ed.), *Archaeology and Coastal Change* (London, 1980). Another useful book which covers many of the subjects dealt with here is B. Jones and D. Mattingly, *An Atlas of Roman Britain* (Oxford, 1990).

A splendid introduction to the Iron Age is provided by the comprehensive and authoritative work by B. Cunliffe, *Iron Age Communities in Britain* (3rd edn. London, 1990). How to manage an Iron Age farm is described by Peter Reynolds, *Iron Age Farm: The Butser Experiment* (London, 1979). Some of the individual sites in the south, mentioned in the text, can be read about more fully: G. Bersu, 'Excavations at Little Woodbury, Wiltshire, part I', *Proceedings of the Prehistoric Society*, 6 (1940), 3–111; G.J. Wainwright, *Gussage All Saints: An Iron Age Settlement in Dorset* (London, 1979) and G.J. Wainwright, 'The excavation of a Durotrigian farmstead near Tollard Royal in Cranborne Chase, southern England', *Proceedings of the Prehistoric Society*, 34 (1968), 102–47. In Wales, the characteristic site at Walesland Rath has not been fully published but a brief account by G.J. Wainwright is contained in *Current Archaeology*, 12 (1968), 4–7. In the north much survey and excavation was carried out on both native and Roman sites, including West Brandon (*Archaeologia Aeliana*[4], 40/1962, 1–34) by the late George Jobey, who published an extensive series of articles in *Archaeologia Aeliana*. An excellent summary, although now dated, is contained in C. Thomas (ed.), *Rural Settlement in Roman Britain* (London, 1966), in which are also conveniently gathered papers on other parts of the country.

The subject of hillforts is very large, but is perhaps most conveniently covered by two works by A.H.A. Hogg: *Hill-forts of Britain* (London, 1975) and *British Hill-forts: An Index* (Oxford, 1979). The type site is now probably Danebury (Hants.), where Barry Cunliffe has carried out not only a long series of excavations, but also a study of the neighbourhood. The results have been published in two volumes: B. Cunliffe, *Danebury, an Iron Age Hill-fort in Hampshire. Vol. 1, The Excavations, 1969–78: The Site* (London, 1984) and *Vol. 2, The Excavations, 1969–78: The Finds* (London, 1984) Oppida have been dealt with comprehensively by B. Cunliffe and T. Rowley (eds), *Oppida in Barbarian Europe* (Oxford, 1976) and more recently by J. Collis, *Oppida* (Sheffield, 1984), which contains many continental examples. Finally for the Iron Age, the Ordnance Survey, *Map of Southern Britain in the Iron Age* (Chessington, 1962) is invaluable in including a short section on communications.

The standard general book on Roman Britain is by S.S. Frere, *Britannia* (London, 1999) now in its 4th edn. Also integral to the subject is the map by the Ordnance Survey, *Roman Britain* (4th edn, Southampton, 1994). Many of the sites mentioned in the text are best seen from the air and S.S. Frere and J.K.S. St Joseph, *Roman Britain from the Air* (Cambridge, 1983) deals with all the major ones. The fortified beach-head at Richborough was first excavated in the 1930s, but not fully published until 1968: B. Cunliffe (ed.), *Fifth Report on the Excavations of the Roman Fort at Richborough, Kent* (Oxford, 1968).

The legionary fortress at Colchester was not discovered until the 1960s. Subsequent excavations, which uncovered a larger area, are published in P. Crummy, *Excavations at Lion Walk, Balkerne Lane, and Middleborough, Colchester, Essex* (Colchester, 1984). The defences of other early legionary fortresses and auxiliary forts of the Claudio-Neronian and Flavian-Trajanic periods are conveniently collected in M.J. Jones, *Roman Fort Defences to AD 117* (Oxford, 1975), while internal arrangements of a selection of forts in the empire of all periods is contained in M. Hassall, 'The internal planning of Roman auxiliary forts', in B. Hartley and J. Wacher (eds), *Rome and her Northern Provinces* (Stroud, 1983). Cavalry regiments are specifically dealt with in two sources: A Hyland, *Equus: The Horse in the Roman World* (London, 1990), and K.R. Dixon and P. Southern, *The Roman Cavalry* (London, 1992), while the cavalry fort at Cirencester is covered in J. Wacher and A. McWhirr, *Early Roman Occupation at Cirencester* (Cirencester, 1982).

The military timber supply has been the subject of some dispute: W.S. Hanson, 'The Roman military timber supply', in *Britannia*, 9 (1978), 293–306, and also J. Wacher, *Roman Britain* (Stroud, 1998), 193–4. The fortress at Inchtuthil generated most arguments; the excavations are published in L.F. Pitts and J.K. St Joseph, *Inchtuthil: The Roman Legionary Fortress* (London, 1985), to which can also be added a logistical survey by E.A.M. Shirley, 'The building of the legionary fortress at Inchtuthil', in *Britannia*, 27 (1996), 111–28. Roman surveying in general is dealt with by O.A.W. Dilke, *The Roman Land Surveyors* (Newton Abbot, 1971) and is as useful in other contexts as in this.

The topography of the two northern frontiers is provided by the two handbooks and by the corresponding Ordnance Survey maps: J. Collingwood Bruce, *Handbook to the Roman Wall* (13th edn, by C.M. Daniels, Newcastle, 1978) and Ordnance Survey, *Hadrian's Wall* (Southampton, 1964); A.S. Robertson, *The Antonine Wall* (Glasgow, 1979) and Ordnance Survey, *The Antonine Wall* (Southampton, 1969).

The Saxon Shore forts are collected together in S. Johnson, *The Roman Forts of the Saxon Shore* (London, 1976), but a good deal of work since then has rendered it somewhat dated. A more recent, but not so comprehensive, handbook is V.A. Maxfield (ed.), *The Saxon Shore: A Handbook* (Exeter, 1989). A remarkable piece of detective work was carried out at Lympne, in order to restore the shape of the fort: B. Cunliffe, 'Excavations of the Roman fort at Lympne', *Britannia*, 11 (1980), 227–88.

Land clearance needed tools and the wide variety that existed are brought together by S.E. Rees, *Agricultural Implements in Prehistoric and Roman Britain* (Oxford, 1979), *vol. I* is descriptive, *vol. II* is a catalogue. The same author has produced a later summary in J. Wacher (ed.), *The Roman World, Vol. II* (London, 1987), 481–503. An earlier source is K.D. White, *Agricultural Implements of the Roman World* (Cambridge, 1967). A clear, descriptive account of all types of field systems is still H.C. Bowen, *Ancient Fields* (London, n.d.). Lists of plants growing in Roman Britain are contained below in the Appendix (p. 130–32). Villas in the western empire are considered in a historical manner by J. Percival, *The Roman Villa* (London, 1976). Edited collections of papers are provided by A.L.F. Rivet (ed.), *The Roman Villa in Britain* (London, 1969) and M. Todd (ed.), *Studies in the Romano-British Villa* (Leicester, 1978). The system as a whole, and the way it functioned, are considered in K. Branigan and D. Miles, *The Economics of Romano-British Villas* (Sheffield, 1988). There is an excellent account of a Roman garden in B. Cunliffe, *Fishbourne: A Roman Palace and its Garden* (London, 1971), while the development of gardens in the Roman Empire has been discussed by L. Farrar, *Ancient Roman Gardens* (Stroud, 1998). Hedges have received little attention; it is therefore interesting to note M. Robinson, 'The Problems of Hedges enclosing Roman and Earlier Fields', in H. C. Bowen and P. J. Fowler (eds)., *Early Land Allotment* (Oxford, 1978), 155–8.

All types of barrows and mausolea in the Roman Empire have been considered by J.M.C. Toynbee, *Death and Burial in the Roman World* (London, 1973), while the British examples have been collected in a paper by R. Jessup, 'Barrows and walled cemeteries in Roman Britain' *Journal of the British Archaeological Association*[3], 22 (1959), 1–32.

Probably the best source for temples and other forms of religious monuments is W. Rodwell, *Temples, Churches and Religion in Roman Britain, Parts I and II* (Oxford, 1980), although for a collection of plans the earlier book by M.J.T. Lewis, *Temples in Roman Britain* (Cambridge, 1966) runs it close.

When we come to urban topography, there are a number of books of interest: J. Wacher, *The Towns of Roman Britain* (London, 1995); B. Burnham and J. Wacher, *The Small Towns of Roman Britain* (London, 1990), both with their copious plans. G. de la Bédoyère, *Roman Towns in Britain* (London, 1992) contains many reconstruction drawings, while small towns are again the subject in A.E. Brown (ed.), *Roman Small Towns in Eastern England and Beyond* (Oxford, 1995). Closer to the subject of topography is F. Grew and B. Hobley (eds), *Roman Urban Topography in Britain and the Western Empire* (London, 1985). The occupations of the inhabitants are indicated in J. Liversidge, *Britain in the Roman Empire* (London, 1968), chap. 13, while law, education and medicine receive attention in the two preceding chapters; G.H. Stevenson, *Roman Provincial Administration* (Oxford, 1939) looks at wider issues. Also informative is J. Wacher, *Roman Britain* (Stroud, 1998), chap. 8. Medicine and disease are specifically dealt with in R. Jackson, *Doctors and Disease in the Roman Empire* (London, 1988), and in C. Roberts and K. Manchester, *The Archaeology of Disease* (Stroud, 1997). The inscriptions for Silvianus' gold ring are contained in R.G. Collingwood and R.P. Wright, *The Roman Inscriptions of Britain, Vol. I* (Oxford, 1965), 306; S.S. Frere and R.S.O. Tomlin (eds), *The Roman Inscriptions of Britain, Vol. II, 3* (Stroud, 1991), 2422.14 and R.S.O. Tomlin, *Tabellae Sulis* (Oxford, 1988), 8, 98; the last reference also contains some interesting comments on theft (p. 79).

O. Davies, *Roman Mines in Europe* (Oxford, 1935) is still an important source for this subject, to which can now be added J.F. Healey, *Mining and Metallurgy in the Greek and Roman World* (London, 1978). More restricted in scope is A. Woods, 'Mining', in J. Wacher (ed.), *The Roman World* (London, 1987), 611–34, since it deals primarily with the important mines in Spain. A number of publications have been produced on Dolaucothi of which probably P.R. Lewis and G.D.B. Jones, 'The Dolaucothi gold mines: the surface evidence', *Antiquaries Journal*, 49 (1969), 244–72, and B.C. Burnham, 'Roman mining at Dolaucothi: the implications of the 1991–3 excavations near the Carreg Pumsaint', *Britannia*, 28 (1997), 325–36 are the most recent.

Perhaps the most informative book on the iron industry is H. Cleere and D. Crossley, *The Iron Industry of the Weald* (Leicester, 1985), since it places the Roman period in its historical context, whereby it can be compared with both earlier and later workings. The Roman period alone is covered in H. Cleere, 'The Roman iron industry in the Weald and its connection with the Classis Britannica', *Archaeological Journal*, 131 (1975), 171–99. The use of all metals in antiquity is comprehensively dealt with by R.F. Tylecote, *A History of Metallurgy* (London, 1976).

The literature on pottery has tended to concentrate on manufacture and marketing, but a glimpse of a working pottery is provided by G.B. Dannell and J.P. Wild, *Longthorpe II: A Military Works Depot* (London, 1987). For a distribution of pottery-making sites see B. Jones and D. Mattingly, *An Atlas of Roman Britain* (Oxford, 1990), 206–7. Brick and tile manufacture are covered by G. Brodribb, *Roman Brick and Tile* (Gloucester, 1987), and by a collection of papers edited by A. McWhirr, *Roman Brick and Tile* (Oxford, 1979), while the extraction and use of salt is the subject of another collection of papers edited by K. de Brisay and K.A. Evans, *Salt: The Study of an Ancient Industry* (Colchester, 1975).

Stone quarries have seldom been investigated archaeologically, and it is a subject still requiring attention. A distribution map of different types of stone is provided by B. Jones and D. Mattingly, *An Atlas of Roman Britain* (Oxford, 1990), 219. An informative source on the different types of stone employed by the Romans all over Britain is J.P. Sedgley, *The Roman Milestones of Britain* (Oxford, 1975), while the art of the stonemason and his tools is comprehensively dealt with by T.F.C. Blagg, 'Tools and techniques of the Roman stonemason in Britain', *Britannia*, 7 (1976), 152–72. Another useful book, which covers building and quarrying in Britain from the Roman to medieval periods, is D. Parsons (ed.), *Stone* (London, 1990).

A very thorough study of the sources of coal used in Roman Britain has recently been provided by A.H.V. Smith, 'Provenance of coals from Roman sites in England and Wales', *Britannia*, 28 (1997), 297–324. The results of an experiment in charcoal burning have been published by T. Clark, 'A charcoal burn and attempt at smelting iron with an open bowl furnace', *Bulletin of the Experimental Firing Group*, 5 (1986–7). The Welwyn bath-house experiments have been published by A. Rook, 'The development and operation of Roman hypocausted baths', *Journal of Archaeological Science*, 5 (1978), 269–82, while the London writing tablet is reported by R.S.O. Tomlin, 'A five-acre wood in Roman Kent', in J. Bird, M. Hassall and H. Sheldon (eds), *Interpreting Roman London* (Oxford, 1996), 209–16.

A more detailed chronology for Roman Britain can be obtained from a choice of sources of which S.S. Frere, *Britannia* (London, 1999) is, as mentioned above, the standard work.

There has been a considerable amount of reconstruction of Roman buildings in recent years in response to the demand to interest the general public. The validity of these is considered in P.J. Drury (ed.), *Structural Reconstruction* (Oxford, 1982) and is particularly useful for containing a paper by B. Hobley, 'Roman military structures at the "Lunt" Roman fort: experimental simulations 1966–77'. Of a similar nature is recent work at Birdoswald where examples of military fortifications have been simulated: R. Birley, *Vindolanda* (London, 1977). As already stressed, many sites are best seen from the air and S.S. Frere and J.K.S. St Joseph, *Roman Britain from the Air* (Cambridge, 1983) is an excellent collection of photographs with appropriate commentaries. The subject of Roman roads is explored by the magisterial survey of I.D. Margary, *Roman Roads in Britain* (London, 1967).

Many of the sites mentioned in the last chapter are in the guardianship of English Heritage, or their Scottish or Welsh equivalents. All these have excellent, informative and accurate guide-books which can be purchased on site or at a nearby museum. Other sites are covered by one or more of the references already given above. Useful general guide-books, which refer to both standing and buried remains, are: R.J.A. Wilson, *A Guide to the Roman Remains in Britain* (London, 1975) and P. Somerset Fry, *Roman Britain* (Newton Abbot, 1984); the latter contains a gazetteer.

APPENDIX

This is a list of common plant species from York, obtained from the General Accident and Rougier Street sites in the colonia; all belong to the Roman period (A.R. Hall and H.K. Kenward, *Environmental Evidence from the Colonia*, York, 1990). Their presence in the list does not necessarily mean that all were growing in York, since the material may have been brought in from some distance away in the countryside. Neither is the list comprehensive. Names in brackets are probably imports, while *names are possibly Roman introductions. The inclusion of 'species' in a name infers that specific identification was not possible.

Trees and shrubs

(Silver Fir)
Willow species
(Walnut)
Dwarf birch
Hazel
(Black mulberry)
Crab apple
Blackthorn
Bullace
Holly
Ash
Elder

Scots Pine
Poplar species
Birch species
Alder
Oak species
(Fig)
Common hawthorn
Wild plum
Sour cherry
(Box)
(Olive)

Other plants

Bog myrtle
Common nettle
Knotgrass
Common persicaria
Sheeps sorrel
Curled dock
Sharp dock
Broad-leafed dock
Bladder campion
White campion
Marsh marigold
Pale hairy buttercup

(Hemp)
Small nettle
Common bistort
Pale persicaria
Water blinks
Thyme-leaved sandwort
Chickweed
Greater chickweed
Lesser Stitchwort
Mouse-ear species
Corn spurrey
Ragged robin

Small-flowered buttercup
Celery-leaved crowfoot
Common meadow rue
Long rough-headed poppy
Flix-weed
Shepherd's purse
Marsh pennywort
Cow parsley
Shepherd's needle
*Coriander
Ground elder
Common water dropwort
Parsley water dropwort
Fine-leaved water dropwort
Fool's parsley
*Fennel
*Dill
Hemlock
Wild celery
Procumbent marsh-wort
Hogweed
Hedge parsley
Wild carrot
Cross-leaved heath
Purple heather
Ling
Marsh andromeda
Bilberry species
Red clover
Flax
Purging flax
(Vine)
Forget-me-not species
Skull cap species
Hemp nettle species
Sea beet
Many seeded goosefoot
Sowbane
White bryony
Woundwort species
Alternate-leaved water milfoil
Self-heal
Goat's beard
Prickly sowthistle
Common sowthistle
Fen sowthistle
Dandelion species

Corn cockle
Lesser spearwort
*Opium poppy
Fumitory species
Marsh yellow cress
Common penny cress
*Turnip
Charlock
Wild radish
Dyer's rocket
Meadow sweet
Raspberry
Blackberry
Common agrimony
Great burnet
Salad burnet
Marsh cinquefoil
Silverweed
Common tormentil
Creeping cinquefoil
Wild strawberry
Parsley piert
Hairy tare
Black medick
Small medick
Strawberry-headed clover
Lesser yellow trefoil
Cowslip
Scarlet pimpernel
Bogbean
Goose grass
Bugle
Common mallow
St John's Wort species
Violet species
Fig-leaved goosefoot
Fat hen
Orache species
Dead nettle species
Cat mint
Mare's tail
Savory
Gypsy-wort
Mint species
Deadly nightshade
Henbane
Black nightshade

Nipple-wort
Hawk's-beard species
Water plantain species
Sea arrow-grass
Pondweed species
Rattle species
Great plantain
Hoary plantain
Ribwort plantain
Danewort
Lamb's lettuce species
Valerian
Lesser valerian
Scabious species
Bell-flower species
Daisy
Sea aster
Bur-marigold species
Stinking camomile
Yarrow
Oxeye daisy
Groundsel species
Burdock species
Thistle species
Knapweed
Sea club-rush
Bulrush
Bristle scirpus
Common spike-rush
Many-stemmed spike-rush

Woody nightshade
Brooklime
Eyebright species
Red rattle
Yellow flag
Heath rush
Salt mud rush
Toad rush
Sharp-flowered rush
Jointed rush
Wood-rush species
Annual meadow grass
Sweet grass species
Brome grass species
Spelt
Bread wheat
Barley species
Common wild oat
Oat
Bent species
Foxtail species
Duckweed species
Bur-reed species
Sedge species
Cat's-ear species
Hawkbit species
Bristly ox-tongue
Cotton grass
Fen sedge
Common sedge

Some other sites have also produced evidence. Among them might be mentioned: Tarraby Lane on Hadrian's Wall near Stanwix (G.H. Smith, 'Excavations at Tarraby Lane', *Britannia*, 9 (1978), 54–7) which provides evidence of both Lime and Elm species, as well as many plant species already listed. London has provided additional information both from the City (P. Marsden, *The Roman Forum Site in London*, London, 1987) and from Southwark (P. Hinton (ed.), *Excavations in Southwark 1973–6 and Lambeth 1973–9*, London, 1988). The former site has provided the Lentil, almost certainly imported, while Southwark can add Cornflower, Black bindweed, Cabbage species, Pea, *Cucumber, Yellow rattle and (Millet). The excavations on the Silchester amphitheatre (M. Fulford, *The Silchester Amphitheatre*, London, 1989) have added Maple, Beech and Ivy to the list of tree species. Colchester has produced Emmer (P. Crummy, *Excavations at Lion Walk, Balkerne Lane and Middleborough*, Colchester 1984).

Much more attention is now being paid to environmental evidence from excavations, and there are a number of other sites with lists of plant remains or pollen, but none as comprehensive as York. But soon it should be possible to create a full botanical list for Roman Britain.

INDEX